"From the very first day of cancer diagnosis, this was not to be a walk in the park for any doctor or patient. Evans and Krivak tell the story of that walk in a frank, candid and semi-humorous way that's very different from the usual 'feel-sorry-for-me' scenarios. This is a must- read book that gives a positive look at a negative situation."

JOHN BARTIMOLE
President, Western New York Healthcare Association,
Buffalo/Niagara New York Area

"Truly a trip. Susan's storytelling has a chatty cadence that keeps us moving swiftly with her on her journey. Like a tour guide, she expertly points out what we should know about the destination and how to get there. Susan tucks her tips and truths into every personal aspect of her diagnosis and treatment. She does this with a healthy mix of humor, emotion, empowerment and, ultimately, hope."

EMILIE DAVIS
S.I. Newhouse School of Public Communications
Syracuse University

"Don't Write the Obituary Yet is a powerful read. Susan captures the raw emotion that people experience when going through a traumatic event such as she did with ovarian cancer. Her candid telling of her own ordeal likely can help others faced with similar situations."

MIKE RYAN
President, Ryan Media Consultants
Vice president (ret.) *The Arizona Republic*
Author of *The Boom! Boom! Book-Practical Tips to
Make Sure Your Career Doesn't Go Bust!*

"The personal experiences and insights Evans shares alongside the expertise of Dr. Krivak help peel away confusion about ' decision making and lend hope to those navigating through journey. It is with wit, wisdom and candor th details and the larger picture of cancer, from an unexpected recovery in this engaging pag

Cancer survivor and Research Managing Editor at the May

Don't Write
THE OBITUARY YET!

Susan Evans

SUSAN EVANS

with Thomas C. Krivak, M.D.

WORD ASSOCIATION PUBLISHERS
www.wordassociation.com
1.800.827.7903

Printed in the United States of America.

ISBN: 978-1-59571-975-1
Library of Congress Control Number: 2014903025

Cover Illustration by
Michelle H. Chapman

Layout/Design by
Jason Price

Published by
Word Association Publishers
205 Fifth Avenue
Tarentum, Pennsylvania 15084

www.wordassociation.com
1.800.827.7903

Each year an estimated 22,240 women are diagnosed with ovarian cancer and approximately 14,030 women will die from this disease.

The physicians and researchers caring for women with this disease appear to be making progress and more women are able to live with this disease. This book hopefully will provide support for families and patients who are in this journey and it may give them a laugh when needed.

Proceeds from the sale of this book will be donated to the Evans-Krivak Gynecological Cancer Research and Education Fund. This fund will support gynecologic cancer research with the goal of improving patients' quality of life as well as search for improved treatments leading to early detection and improved survival.

Donations to this fund can be made online at:

www.pittsburghfoundation.org/give a donation or sent directly to **the Pittsburgh Foundation**, Five PPG Place, Suite 250, Pittsburgh, PA 15222-5414 restricted to the grant provision of the Evans-Krivak Gynecological Cancer Research and Education Fund.

No man is an island.
Each is a piece of the continent
A part of the main.
If a clod be washed away by the sea,
Europe is the less.
As well as if a promontory were.
As well as if a manner of thine own
Or of thine friend's were.
Each man's death dimishes me,
For I am involved in mankind.
Therefore, send not to know
For whom the bell tolls.
It tolls for thee

—*John Donne*

Contents

To My Parents
Michael and Virginia Cavalline
Who Gave Me Life

To Thomas C. Krivak, M.D.
Who Saved My Life

To My Husband
George P. Evans, Ph.D.
Who Is My Life

I'm not afraid of storms
I'm learning how to sail my ship

—Louisa May Alcott

*The authors would like to thank the Blaisdell Foundation
For helping to make this work possible.*

Foreword

As a gynecologic oncologist, I am pleased to collaborate with Susan Evans as her doctor and coauthor on her ovarian cancer journey. She provides uncanny humor and insight for patients needing comfort as they face this highly deceptive disease.

She describes her journey from a rural hospital to an urban one, revealing the challenges among the arsenal of quality care in a complex medical system. She cannot say enough about the importance of caring medical professionals and their influence on recovery.

Just as doctors raise questions to patients, Sue flips that around by very strongly advising patients to question their entire medical team. That questioning is not only a patient's right but also an inseparable part of a patient's responsibility for quality care.

In a light-hearted yet serious way, Sue minces no words in an extraordinary recollection of a diagnosis that started out as a swollen ankle and ended as ovarian cancer.

Her story, with her in my thoughts and at her side along the journey, is quite a revelation, indeed.

Thomas C. Krivak, MD

Preface

Cancer is not a trip for which you necessarily plan. You can't use your vacation points, or trade your timeshare week, or book a flight. It just happens. You don't get a trip-tic from AAA, you can't program your GPS system, and you won't be printing a Mapquest sheet off your computer. You're on your own to find your way. It probably won't be a pleasant trip, but you may find at the end of it that you have learned a lot about cancer, life, your family, your friends, and most of all, yourself. So you could consider it one of those educational trips that you see advertised on TV. You'll think that you're in a foreign country: the language spoken certainly isn't anything you readily recognize, the activities will be new to you and the myriad of people will make you think you have crossed over to a not-so-amusing amusement park line.

It's a trip that starts out suddenly and unexpectedly. There's no packing for it. You just go.

I am going to share my trip with you. You may never have to go on this trip by yourself, at least I hope not. But you may find that sharing my trip will help you to not only know more about this disease and all of the peripheral challenges that accompany it, but to empathize with those you know who have made the trip. But as I said, if this is your trip, you will know so much more about yourself and what you really can deal with.

The trip won't be taken alone. You'll have family and friends, you will have neighbors and even people you never met up to this point who will help you along the way. You won't get lost. You will have doctors, nurses, technicians, physician assistants—all who will help you take each step on this trip. Don't worry when you lose your way because they'll pick up the map and show you where you went wrong.

On a hot night—June13, 2012 to be exact—I began my trip of a lifetime.

The 25 - Pound Tumor

Cancer. There, now we've said it. It's the one word that neither men nor women ever want to hear.

It's like George Carlin's seven words you can't say on radio and TV (although I do think I have heard some of those words recently—you may even read one or two of them in this book). If you're of my generation you know what a stir those words caused. But cancer is a word we hear every day. We read about the disease, we see commercials on TV for the cancer institutes. We are told about various symptoms, for just about everything relating to it, but we don't want to hear that word when it refers to us. The day the doctor called me and told me that "yes, it was cancer" and that he wanted me to start chemotherapy as soon as possible, was the worst day in my life. I was thinking, OK, this is it, better get the laundry done and the bills paid.

Cancer is not a new disease, but it is new when you are directly involved in it—not as a bystander helping a friend, a relative, a co-worker or a neighbor—but as the object of the dreaded disease.

It does not discriminate, it is an equal opportunity disease and it cannot be fixed overnight.

There I was, one hot June night, looking at an ER computer screen showing me the results of my CTscan. I had gone to the doctor's earlier that day with a swollen ankle, and a few hours later I was being told that I had what looked like a 25-pound tumor! Now, if I would have had any reasoning ability at the time, the 25-pound tumor would have sounded absolutely ridiculous. But what could I do in a hospital gown and no shoes? I couldn't run (although at one point in my life, a month into our marriage, I had walked out of this very same hospital in my nightgown. That's when I was sure that my husband thought that being married to me would be a long road). However, the ER doctor was so serious, he went to medical school, not I, that perhaps the enormity of the tumor could be true.

A 25- POUND TUMOR, THAT'S THE SIZE OF A THANKSGIVING TURKEY...

A 25- pound tumor, that's the size of a Thanksgiving turkey, or my Sheltie, or a sack of flour that could make 50 pizzas. OK, it does sound a bit nuts at that.

Besides this "turkey" that is growing inside of me, the doctor also was telling me that my blood sugar was disastrously high. No more bread, pasta (being Italian I was starting to see the end of the world as I knew it). No sugar or sweets, what was left? (Did this doctor work for Weight Watchers?) I envisioned my library of cookbooks being sold at a garage sale.

Just about at this point I wanted to say F---! But I couldn't: small town, everyone knows me, retired local high school English teacher, member of several boards, etc. (Oh, George Carlin! Where are you?)

So, that turkey's in there. I can't eat anything ever again. I can't yell the best stress-relieving word that was ever invented and the doctor is strongly suggesting that I go to the Roswell Cancer Institute in Buffalo, NY. I looked at my husband who had the deer in the headlights look and we both were thinking, "Holy Shit"!

SUSAN EVANS

Now, the Roswell Cancer Institute is an excellent, nationally known, cancer research facility. Only an hour and a half drive from our home. No problem. But when you have to select a facility of this type you must keep in mind a few practical points. At this point I had no time to go home and do research. Because I had blood clots in my leg I wasn't permitted to go home at all. So I quickly ran a checklist in the part of my mind that was still working. Where will I be most comfortable? What do I know about the staff and the hospital's reputation? Where will my husband and friends stay? It sounded like I would be there longer than a day—as it turned out, nine days to be exact.

Medical professionals always say not to make hasty decisions, but sometimes that's all the time you have. I said "no" to the Roswell idea, and of course our rural hospital could not handle the 25-pound tumor which they had diagnosed. I had to select a hospital and select one quickly. Being born and raised in Pittsburgh, which I still consider to be my home, it took but one breath to say UPMC Magee Women's Hospital. Eyebrows raised in the ER. Apparently they were pro-Buffalo (but what self-respecting Steelers' fan would choose Buffalo?)

...AND REMEMBER THAT IT IS YOUR DECISION...

No one told me that selecting my hospital was only one of the many steps in this trip. But at least I had made the one important decision—and remember that it is YOUR decision, no one else's.

The ability to make that decision gave me a small sense of empowerment. Always remember that even though you have a condition that is very serious and that you may not understand, you always can make the decisions. It's up to you.

As my husband and I tried to process this medical "news" we felt better that we could go to where we were most comfortable and where we knew the city. He just looked at me and left the decision to me—it was my life and what did he know about women's hospitals? I was sure at that point that a woman's hospital would take good care of women—that's what they do. I was not disappointed.

If you have the time, you and your doctor should evaluate which hospital would be best for you. Some hospitals may be better equipped and some have expertise in dealing with specific problems. All hospitals are not equal, no matter what they want you to think.

As patients, we probably do not realize that it is not just the doctor but the entire team who will get us well. From the moment I arrived at Magee I found the "team" approach to be in working order. I was surrounded by people who just wanted me to be comfortable (and to stop crying).

SUSAN EVANS

When evaluating a facility you will want to know the hospital's experience in treating people with your condition, the quality rating they have received for any procedures you need, and their record for keeping the patient safe. Thankfully, all of this can be found on the Internet without too much trouble. But keep in mind that not everything on the Internet is as accurate as we think and if you have the time you should do more extensive research. Even though you may select a hospital and a specific doctor you always can change your mind. Don't worry about hurting someone's feelings—they have plenty of patients. Make sure that **you** are the patient for **them**.

I did not have much of a choice, but the choice I did make turned out to be the correct one.

Choosing the right doctor might be another choice that you have the chance to make. Check on his experience, where does he have admitting privileges, his gender (you may feel more comfortable with a female doctor), his communication style, his credentials, and the all-important issue of insurance coverage.I did not have the choice of doctors, one was assigned, and luckily that was the right one for me.

Actually getting to my choice was another adventure.

I had an overnight stay in the local hospital, not the best experience, no private rooms available that night. When I was in college I never was very enthusiastic about dorm life. Staying with another stranger in a room and sharing a bathroom weren't on my priority list. So there I was in a rural hospital next to a stranger and wondering what would happen next. I thought back over the past six months. I had been diagnosed first with a foot problem which could be helped by purchasing inserts for my shoes. I was told that maybe I had phlebitis. Then it was elastic stockings that would cure the problem of the swelling in my ankle. Then it was off to the chiropractor who immediately knew that this was no back problem. By now you should be able to hear, as I could, the sound of the cash register each time there was a missed diagnosis.

Off I went for the blood clot test—none.

The CA125 for ovarian cancer had already been done—none. Why couldn't any medical professional pinpoint this problem? It all seems so easy on the television shows, *ER or Grey's Anatomy*. They can diagnose, cure, and send you home all in about 35 minutes. Why can't life be like that?

I waited all of the next day until an ambulance could be summoned to take me to Pittsburgh. My friends came to the hospital, trying to offer encouragement, always with tears in their eyes. I imagined they all were looking for their black dresses just in case!

Never having been in an ambulance in my life I had no idea what a real treat this was going to be. If you have ever driven the roads from Northwestern Pennsylvania to Pittsburgh you know that the state budget hasn't allowed a lot of funds to be spent on paving. As I bounced around for three hours, tethered to my IV, I almost could feel the bruises being created on my body. By the time I got to Magee I was sure that they would think not only does this person have cancer but she also must be a victim of spousal abuse.

And where was that spouse anyhow? He was speeding through the city of Pittsburgh at 10p.m. frantically looking for this hospital. GPS systems are only good if you are in a city that doesn't change the road signs and put up detours seemingly every day. He arrived shortly after the ambulance. He later told me that while he was driving he also was planning my funeral—pall bearers were selected in his mind, venue was chosen and the musical selections were also being considered. Since the local hospital had implied that I was in a very dangerous situation with but a few months to live, my husband felt that pre-planning was a good idea. Having this type of concern was heartening, if he could plan the funeral while driving I supposed that he would be able to handle most anything that would occur. It also gave me something to laugh about later in the journey.

Now I thought this was stretching the planning a bit, but at least he was thinking of something that needed done. No last-minute planning for us.

Was it really a 25-pound tumor? Of course not. There's a big difference between 25 and 2.5. Was my sugar level off the Richter charts—of course not—it was 107 (just about everyone knows that your sugar level may go up due to stress).

And that's just one reason that we need higher math standards in this country!

The First Few Days

There I was in the hospital bed thinking back on what I had thought was an almost perfect life—only child, loving parents, made it through the '60s without being arrested or addicted, financially secure, wonderful husband, retired from a wonderful teaching job, rarely sick. Other than having my tonsils out when I was six years old, and having my wisdom teeth removed, I had only spent one adult night in the hospital for dehydration. So what did I know about this hospital business? Other than a few doctors with whom I was acquainted, I didn't even know anyone who worked in a hospital! That might have been a blessing in disguise.

My first morning at Magee was my first step on the medical learning curve. The clock ticked on to about 10a.m.—no

even mentioned. Okay, maybe this was
ı therapy. Maybe that 25-pound tumor
f they didn't feed me. Highly unlikely,
:akfast? Finally, not wanting to cause
:han they obviously had, I asked an aide
:all and order what you wanted off the
menu?" WHAT menu? There it was on the bedside table.

A menu—maybe this place really was as good as I thought.
Perhaps one of Pittsburgh's finest restaurants had opened up a
hospital franchise? Was this food going to show up on my bill
marked as "room service"? At this point I didn't care.

My mind then backtracked to the previous night when I
arrived at the hospital. As I was wheeled from the ambulance
I was on a lovely balcony overlooking a beautiful lobby complete with a grand piano. Does someone rate hospitals like
they do hotels? If they do, this one definitely gets five stars.
Not only did it look like a place from which I may not try to
escape, but it was high-tech. As I was wheeled to my room,
late that night, no one was around and a deafening silence
ruled the halls. But what was this thing I saw? There it was,
a rather large filing cabinet decorated with Steelers' pictures
(right team for me). Now, I was either hallucinating or going
crazy but that cabinet was traveling up and down the empty
hall by itself! A robotic filing cabinet! I later was told that this
robot delivered medications and other medical supplies. The

personnel found that at times it often was cheaper and more reliable than a real person.

Once I got the hang of the meals and how to walk to the bathroom while tethered to the Heparin IV and the heart monitor, then things were starting to settle down. Other than me crying every five minutes (fear will do that to you) I was starting to feel like someone had made a terrible mistake and I really was fine and would be going home before dinner was ordered.

My husband had begun the vigil, computer in hand and we were waiting to meet this person named Krivak whose name was on my door.

Some of the resident doctors had been in to make me feel at home—lovely young women who were dedicating their lives to medicine. They were friendly and immediately wanted to know how I had been so lucky to get this Krivak person. They sang his praises and felt that he was one of the best. They also threw in their opinion that he was one of the best-dressed doctors in the hospital. (Being much older than these young women I wondered how jeans and a sweater would put this doctor in the best-dressed category. If this was the truth, what did the other doctors wear? Sweats and t-shirts? Later in my journey I did get to see what they were referring to. The first time that I had an appointment in the doctor's office he came in dressed—shirt, tie, cuff links, the whole deal. They weren't wrong after all.)

Later, one of my friends said that I had not gotten this doctor by chance but there was some Divine intervention involved. She suggested that my parents, who were deceased, and who I hoped were not planning on reuniting with me so soon, had made sure that I was assigned one of Pittsburgh's top-rated surgeons.

Of course, my mind ran to, maybe I have such a serious problem that they were sending in the big guns!

All of this wouldn't matter since I was still hoping that my being there was a mistake. I was sure that I would be home shortly. I was sure that someone had confused my x-rays with another patient's, or had mislabeled my lab tests—it was time to go home and forget this whole ordeal.

...HE WAS A STEELERS' FAN I GUESSED I COULD KEEP HIM.

However, I soon learned there was no chance of that happening.

The day wore on, a bit of a nap and when I opened my eyes there he was. Now let's just say that when God made him, he did good! There stood this young man at the foot of my bed in his scrubs and a Pittsburgh Steelers' surgery cap. I was sure that I hadn't died and that this wasn't an archangel and since he was a Steelers' fan I guessed I could keep him. However, were medical schools now taking kids when they were 10 years old, because this guy didn't look old enough to have graduated. Maybe he was one of those child prodigies.

It is often said that you can judge a person by a first impression—so I thought I would wait and see what he said, how he said it and if I thought that he was the doctor for me. (You can always ask for someone else, so don't be intimidated when you are lying in that hospital gown. Speak up!)

Now, when was the last time that a doctor asked you if he could sit down? In my case, never. I have never found doctors to have the best manners and I have never felt safe with doctors—too many bad experiences with that profession, I guess. They always, in my experience, were clinical, cold and businesslike-no time for the patient. But here he was asking me if he could sit down. Obviously this "boy" (aren't they all just that) had been raised right, manners and all. My feelings toward doctors, at least this one, were quickly turning around.

It's strange, but looking back at this moment I often felt that in some way I was "cheated."

SUSAN EVANS

Being an educated woman, and considering myself rather "with it," I often felt that I should have had the advantages of the modern digital world and that I should have had the time to research this cancer, this staff and this doctor. He could have been one of Pittsburgh's worst instead of one of its best, how did I know? As I have said, I did not have the advantage of doing the research or even thinking about the situation. Would it have made any difference? Probably not, but that cheated feeling remains with me to this day, even though no amount of research could have found me a better doctor.

Feeling safe and secure with your doctor is going to be very important in this journey. He has your life in his hands and you can't do too much about that. He makes the map and he charts the course, you need to trust him, like him, and honestly feel that he is going to get you back to good health. Later, as I asked him opinions on treatment options he often said that he wouldn't be telling me to do anything that he wouldn't tell his mother or his sister. Good enough for me.

So here was the man whose name was on the door. Polite, kind and the bearer of bad news. Yes, indeed, it was ovarian cancer, as far as he could tell from the tests and yes there was going to be surgery.

Being a person who expects immediate answers, my questions were: Can you fix it and am I going to die? No one can answer when a person might die but at least I was looking for an answer that did not entail dying during the next few weeks. No matter how intelligent and well-educated you might be—those are the questions that will be foremost in your mind at the onset of this adventure. The answers were simple: "yes," it can be fixed, and "no," you probably won't die this week (at least not from the cancer).

After you are told that you have cancer, life is not over, it just gets much more complicated. If you have never been a person who makes lists or asks questions, now would be a good time to start.

Once you realize how serious this situation is you need to think of a few other things that go into your decision-making process. If you want to only live for today then do nothing—walk out of the doctor's office or hospital, tell no one and live out your days.

...THERE WILL BE HOPE.

Do you want tomorrows? Accept the diagnosis and do the treatments, even though there will be no guarantees, no promises—but there will be hope.

But first there were a few other issues with which to deal. The tests revealed blood clots and before surgery could be done a filter had to be inserted to prevent any movement of the blood clots into my lungs. This long tube was called an inferior vena cava filter and was to be inserted through a vein in my neck. It would sit in the vena cava, a large vein, below the kidneys. This procedure in itself was not as terrible as it sounds but it was uncomfortable. Why is it that the medical profession seems to insist that everything be as annoying as possible? During the procedure my head was turned to one side and a large blue paper sheet was placed over my head—rather claustrophobic to say the least. A nurse kept asking if I was all right and I wanted to say, "get the damned paper sheet off my face and I will feel a lot better." But of course I didn't complain; they were doing their job and I was trying to do mine.

I had asked the doctor ahead of time if this procedure would hurt. Of course he had said "no". He said "just a little pressure"—I have now had the pleasure of realizing that his interpretation of pressure is generally some pain. Perhaps all of these doctors need to undergo these treatments—I bet the patient then would get a better explanation!

The next morning when he and the residents came in to check on me I told one of the women to take out a pen and write what I had to say on her clipboard. They looked wide-eyed at me but one got her pen out, poised to write whatever words of wisdom I was going to bestow.

As the doctor sat on the couch waiting for my comments, I said, "This year at your annual Christmas party make sure that Dr. Krivak gets the bullshit award for telling me the procedure would not hurt."

There was a pregnant pause, those women dared not laugh in front of their mentor, and I heard the good doctor say, "That's more than I got last year!" Having a doctor with a good sense of humor also is helpful during this journey. Since this procedure was completed I felt that we could move on. But of course, that was not the end of it.

Later that day once again my doctor stood at the end of the bed, but with one difference, there was another doctor with him. This man did not seem as young so maybe he was the man in charge. Wrong again, he was the urologist, Dr. T. Jaffe, another wonderful, kind person. (This hospital must have a wonderful HR office because everyone is so nice.) This could only mean big trouble in my mind. Two doctors at once, now what?

Well, the "what" was a kidney stone that they didn't want moved during surgery. To prevent any movement they would place two stents in my kidneys. Here we go again, what did I know? My husband had heart stents. Were these the same things?

Nope—these things were like long, green strands of spaghetti. Never having any procedure done in my life, I of course agreed—they assured me it wouldn't be a big deal—at least not to them.

Now things were really starting to go from bad to worse in my mind. Of course I was assured that these were all minor procedures that could be handled during the next few days.

I guess I would be there for more than one dinner.

My trip had just begun.

The "Flock"

Now that's not the best word to use for the group of young women in their white coats, who arrived at my door daily at 5:45a.m., but it does describe the feeling I got when they first descended upon me. These were the white-coated "sheep" who came without the shepherd most of the time. These young doctors at times are the "heart and soul" with whom patients and families can talk, ask questions and vent their frustrations. Personally, I found it much more satisfying to "vent" directly with the doctor. I'm sure he appreciated that!

As most people know, a hospital is no place to get any sleep. Each night I was awakened by various tech people to draw blood (just how much did they need, and how often, and for what reason?), take blood pressure, and I guess to make sure that I didn't fall out of bed or hadn't unhooked myself from the machines and run out the doors!

So, here they came. Lovely young women, full of compassion, energy and information. It didn't take long to establish some rapport with these ladies and one morning the visit turned into a book club session discussing the current New York Times bestseller, *Fifty Shades of Gray*. It seems like just about every woman had read this novel, and every man should. As we discussed the book, and Ana, and Christian, the main characters, the ladies shared their opinions that my doctor could definitely play the part of Christian in a movie version. I didn't want to ask if they thought he really was like that character. As we discussed this, another doctor, obviously one who was in charge of the group, (another shepherd?), poked his head in the door and asked the ladies if they were ready to move on. I answered and said we were having book club, he laughed and suggested that we wrap up the discussion as quickly as possible. It was nice having young women and doctors who were personable at 5:45 each morning and knowing that I was important for just a few minutes. It was true. The power of laughter and the comfort that these women gave always made me feel better. This hospital knew how important hese qualities are for patient care—all hospitals should.

After my surgery it wasn't all fun—each visit came with one of the women doing a "peek" as she called it. She would check my sutures, heartbeat, all of the usual procedures. The difference from other experiences? This young doctor would first ASK if she could take a look. All so polite. That made it so much easier.

I believe that women look at this medical stuff a bit differently than do men. Personally, I have never been the type of person to shower with other women, or run around a gym half naked. In fact, when I was in high school I always got a "D" in gym. Not because I couldn't do the activities but because I was not about to change or shower in the locker room with the other girls. There's that Catholic school upbringing and the Italian guilt influencing my life!

So this having people look at your naked body was just not in my frame of reference, especially since they all were strangers. I am not sure that male doctors realize how embarrassing, and even humiliating, those internal exams can be. I sometimes thought that maybe these men didn't know as much about women as they should, but that's a whole other male issue, isn't it?

Couldn't someone invent a machine that could do the job just as well? However, there's not much choice when they're trying to make sure you don't die during the next six months. After a while you get used to it.

SUSAN EVANS

MY **SKIN** RESEMBLED THE COLOR OF **MY** JEANS.

Later in my journey, during one of those embarrassing vaginal exams, when I had been living through twice daily Lovonox injections for months, I mentioned to my doctor that both legs and my stomach were as bruised as they could get. My skin resembled the color of my jeans.

He listened and I said, "look at them." He pulled back the sheet, by this time he had seen enough of my naked body for a lifetime, and was a bit surprised. That got me a two-week reprieve from the injections. Speak up, don't just accept without questioning.

You just have to get over the embarrassing part, I guess.

That personal, caring touch of these women certainly helped me accept all of this.

Soon another young woman arrived, looking very tired, up all night I suppose, and started to explain to me what the length of my incision would be after surgery. Again, I felt like that 25-pound "turkey" was reappearing—a very long incision she explained, because no one knew how much room would be needed once the surgery began. Little did I know that the incision would look like a road map from Mapquest when we were done! No future as a senior Victoria's Secret model after this was done.

Through all of this I made myself remember that laughter gets you through most things in life, and that "pride goes before a fall," so I forgot my pride and started to find humor wherever I could.

I did, however, often think of which of the three rivers I would jump into if things got really bad. Alphabetical order always seems the best to me so the Allegheny would be the first!!

Along with these early morning visits came visits from friends, parish priests, old and new (the anointing of the sick just about put my Presbyterian friend into a state), doctors of all kinds, cardiologists, urologists and social workers making sure that everything was all right, just to name a few.

The visits might seem annoying but they help to pass the time and they make you feel cared for—medical people work so hard, and they actually seem to like what they are doing even though they probably haven't had a night's sleep since they entered medical school. Enjoy them as much as you can. Either you control your attitude or it controls you—it's your choice.

In this situation you find that your life can be changed in a matter of hours by people you don't even know. Accept that.

SUSAN EVANS

Keep in mind that prayer of St. Francis that we all seem to know: "*God grant me the serenity to accept things I cannot change. The courage to change the things I can, and the wisdom to know the difference.*"

When you have cancer you cannot change it. Accept the fact that those doctors and nurses will do all they can to help you. Focus on the positive, and don't ask, "Why me?" Accept it, take control and your doctor will do all in his power to have you survive and flourish.

Vocabulary-101

There's a lesson in life that most of us learn early. You don't go to a plumber to fix your car, nor do you go to a painter to pave your driveway. So why do we try to circumnavigate our way around the medical profession? Maybe it's because they don't speak English, and we do.

Remember when you were in school and you didn't understand the terminology in a course? How long did that hour of class-time seem and how much did you care if you learned anything about the material being presented?

I certainly wouldn't expect my doctor to understand Iambic Pentameter, locate the denouement in a story or be able to fill out a plot line. What about Socratic method and the

Aristotilian method of thought in an essay? Would these medical geniuses understand Stream of Consciousness? So why do they assume that we understand what they are telling us? Making a decision about my treatment is much more important to this retired English teacher (who had 24 credits above her Master's Degree) than analyzing Shakespeare, but without the medical vocabulary I didn't know if I was going to survive or if I was playing a game of *Jeopardy* and "Medical Terms" was the category.

DO THEY HAVE ANY IDEA WHAT IT IS LIKE TO BE A PATIENT...

On the day before my surgery my doctor arrived in my room and rattled off a list of things that might occur during surgery and would I give him permission to deal with them as he saw fit? Now let's remember, this is a man I hardly knew who had my life in his hands. Panic-mode was quickly setting in when he started on this list—I remember the word appendix, I knew what that was, but what about ileostomy or removal of the spleen? And then I heard "colostomy."

If I could have breathed at that moment I might have stopped him on that one, but the moment flew by and I agreed to everything. (Had he said liposuction, breast reduction, something useful? Probably not.) Out came the forms, sign here (with the hand that had been attached to the IV for days and could hardly move). Do they have any idea what it is like to be a patient, is there a medical law that says the doctor can't explain something in simple, short syllable words?

The National Center for Educational Statistics in cooperation with the Educational Testing Services conducted a National Adult Literacy Survey (NALS). Taking into account all of the variables which are not necessary for the point that I am trying to make, an adult in the United States reads between the 8th and 9th grade level. Granted, their comprehension levels may be a bit higher, or lower, but 8th grade is 8th grade.

According to these testing services, the 8th-grade level puts someone in the 50th percentile of the 8th grade. The upper levels of the 8th grade will be reading at the 50th percentile of the average 12th grade and the lower levels of the average will be reading at the 50th percentile of the average 4th grade. Now, 4th grade is 4th grade.

A novel is usually written on about the 7th-grade level—that is the level of the John Grisham and Mark Twain books. Some newspapers are printed on a 4th-grade reading level so that the average American can read and understand the content. We are not all average but we all do need to understand what is written or to be able to comprehend what we read or hear.

The point is, the average medical textbook is written on an above 12th-grade level. That is reassuring! Those are the books our doctors study and from which they gain their knowledge. The problem is, they are so used to those levels that they do not seem to realize that their average patient has no idea what the medical terms or concepts mean.

Most people are relatively smart when it comes to their professions and lives, but we are not doctors so we do not understand everything that is being thrown at us in a hospital setting. Those simple, short-syllable words are what we need. I already was impressed with my doctor's medical skills or he wouldn't be my doctor, so now explain so I can understand.

Dr. Jaffe, the urologist, drew pictures to explain the stent locations. Had he taken an art class in medical school? Couldn't all of the doctors take this class?

Surgery is a fear-filled and fearful experience because we are not physicians or surgeons and we do not know what is going to happen to us. Couldn't the staff explain more slowly and thoroughly? Couldn't they realize that when we say we understand something, we really don't. We say we do because we hardly can get many words out of our mouths. That's why it's always good to have someone with you when you're speaking to the doctor. My friend Kathy, an English teacher, was always there with her notebook and pen in hand.

This isn't like your Friday spelling/vocabulary test in school. There is no time to research terms and learn new words.

This really was a learning experience.

I listened to the list of possible problems, my husband at my side, and I just hoped that God was on this shift and that he had his scrubs on and was going to supervise this young doctor. I might not know what these terms meant but God sure did. Now this is when you just start praying to every being you can think of. I believe at this point I even made up a few saints just to hedge my bets. Once you agree to the surgery and the wheels are in motion you need to find peace within yourself.

For me, this was the first time that I really had to come to grips with my own mortality. I had survived my husband being taken by Life Flight to UPMC Hamot in Erie. I had survived my parents' deaths, but now it was me. We all know that sooner or later we will leave this earth—but I never felt the urgent desire to go right now. I thought of a line in a song that I had recently heard, "You never know when he's coming back or when you're leaving." True enough, it would be fine if He came back, but I didn't want to leave just yet.

I STILL HAD A LOT TO DO.

SUSAN EVANS

I still had a lot to do. There were many more Steelers' games that would need my help, more Super Bowls to get to, much more shopping to do. I had to take care of George, the dog, the house. There were books to read, recipes to try, meetings to attend—nope, it wasn't time yet.

Why Me?

It's easy to fall into the trap of asking yourself, "Why me?" Don't ask. Do you ask why you can't seem to have the winning Powerball numbers, ever, or why you can't ever find your car keys when you're in a hurry? There's just some questions that don't need asking because the answers aren't there nor would they be important.

According to the most recent findings of the Surveillance, Epidemiology and End Results (SEER) Program of the National Cancer Institute, the incidence of ovarian cancer in 2012 was 22,280 and the projected deaths were estimated at 15,500. Not very good odds if you ask me. A woman's life-time risk of dying from invasive ovarian cancer is projected at 1 in 95. I can't say that I liked those odds either.

The problem with these projected numbers is that they are "general" figures. The Internet can give us all of the information available, but that information is not specific to you or to me. We all have read or heard about the most common symptoms: bloating, pelvic pain, difficulty eating, urinary frequency, fatigue (aren't most modern women tired?), back pain, pain during sex, to name a few. Nowhere is a swollen ankle listed as a symptom or a blood clot!

...MY DOCTOR WARNED ME AGAINST... DOING INTERNET RESEARCH.

But here I was reading facts that said if I made it through the next five years I would have a 75% survival rate and if I made it through the next 10 years I would have a 34% survival rate. Again, I didn't like those odds, but the facts are the facts.

One thing my doctor warned me against from the start is doing Internet research. Maybe I should have listened. The "facts" aren't me, or you, they're general information. We, on the other hand, are "specific."

So, if you're still here reading this, and you're obviously not dead, then don't ask, "Why me?".

Of course, this is the perfect time to dust off those prayers you used to know, or to meditate on your "higher power" be it Jesus, Mohammed, Buddha, God, or any other supreme being. Nowhere are any of us guaranteed a long and perfect life. Nowhere are we guaranteed the answers to our questions. By asking "Why me?" we are putting ourselves on a very demanding level with a supreme being—and that's probably not where we are supposed to be.

It's hard, almost impossible, to accept a cancer diagnosis. We're all so afraid of this disease that when it takes hold of our lives we dip into a panic mode. No matter who we are or what we have accomplished in our lives, it is painful to hear the doctor say, "You have cancer."

Several times a doctor would enter my room and ask about my family history and who in my family might have died from some form of cancer. I repeated my answer each time, "No one." My immediate family members all died of heart attacks and I had assumed that I would also—and still may. They often looked at me with the "dumb dog" look, as if my recollection of my family history was somehow skewed. No skewing here boys; hearts, not cancer.

What makes all of this easier? What can get you through the first few panic-filled days? The answer would usually be "family," but my husband and I have no family to speak of.

SUSAN EVANS

We have no children, our parents are deceased as are most of our relatives. We are truly alone in this world. That's a daunting situation to be in; without each other life would be almost hermit-like. When faced with this diagnosis we truly felt like the end was near. We have good friends, one of whom told me, "We're in this together." That was good to know but in the dark of night, in a hospital room, you find that you are really in this alone. It's good to have people to support you and to help, but when all is said and done, you're the one being rolled into the operating room and praying that you will awaken and still be in this world.

This is a life-changing event for all who are around you—but mostly it is life changing for you. All of the encouragement—a lot of it seemingly polyannish—can never fill the void in your heart. You will find that you never will regain the peace in your heart that you had before the diagnosis. That's okay, as time goes on you'll find a different kind of peace, a peace that comes from knowing that your doctor is doing all he/she can to keep you healthy.

True contentment is not raising the "why" question.

All of the stories about surgery and chemotherapy race through your head: Will it really be as bad as they say? (Almost) Will it be like TV portrays it? (No) Will I have the strength to do this? (Yes) When I would speak with my doctors I always seemed to mention that my husband has a heart problem and who was going to take care of him while I was going through this? Those of us who are the caregiver type know how frustrating it can be when we cannot give care and have to be the recipients of care instead. One young doctor told me that this is the problem with women, that we always put our families, spouses, careers, and homes ahead of ourselves.

The nights in a hospital can be very long if you can't sleep. That's when the demons arrive at the door and just let themselves into not only your room but into your heart as well. It's easy to give-in to panic when you're alone in the dark.

Those demons arrived at my door the first night at the hospital. My nurse realized this and she sat and talked with me for the longest time. She told me about her son and his musical skills. We talked about education. We pushed the demons into the hall for a time, maybe that robotic filing cabinet would run them over. I cried unceasingly...she kept talking and reassuring me. In the middle of all of this drama I got the idea that if I could have a shower I would feel much better. A shower it was—the staff was taught to aim to please. I finally did get to sleep. The demons did not win that night.

But I Have Season Tickets

Have you noticed in life that all of us put importance on some really inconsequential things? Men might think that their fraternity t-shirt is of historical, educational and genealogical importance. Try to reschedule your husband's golf weekend with his friends and it borders on insurrection. Women are not immune from this either. Losing an earring can ruin a day. Nails not done, hair not cut, hard to even continue through another 24 hours.

My friend's daughter was getting married in the fall and she had purchased her mother-of- the bride-dress. Unfortunately, after the dress was purchased she was diagnosed with a heart problem which would demand heart surgery and valve replacement. She looked at the doctor with tears in her eyes and said, "But I have my dress!" She explained the depth of the neckline and he agreed to put the surgery on hold until after the wedding. There's those priorities.

When faced with a high school crisis, I taught for 32 years, my favorite comment always was,"No one died, did they?" If no one dies when something goes wrong, then how bad can it be? I wasn't dead yet so there was still hope. There is always hope.

"BREATHE IN, BREATHE OUT, MOVE ON."

In our community my husband and I had once purchased a granite bench as a fund -raiser for our Trails Association. Engraved on the bench is the saying, "Nothing is more important than this day." I had to keep this in mind as my encounter with cancer began. One day at a time, a cliche that we all hear, became ever more relevant to me than at this time. Jimmy Buffet captures the idea, "breathe in, breathe out, move on." It's reinforced during your hospital stay because there's no hurrying these people. No use complaining (up until this experience complaining was one of my major "sports" next to shopping). Nothing is going to get done until the hospital staff says it is.

Once I got to Magee and was settled in my room in the brand new section (no surprise to my friends that the "princess" would be in a new wing), it was time for a trip to the imaging lab. Although I had guarded the brown envelope with my imaging results which I was given as I left the local hospital, I quickly was told that only half of the scan had made it with me to Pittsburgh. Apparently the local institution forgot to put the other half in the envelope. So off I went to the lab.

I will never forget Mike who gave me such positive reinforcement. Here I was crying again, as again the fear kicked in. Mike introduced himself (they are all so polite at this place) and he explained the procedure and tried to calm me.

Now, here's where placing importance on trivial things comes into play.

If you're from Pittsburgh and you're a Steelers' fan (how could you not be?) one of your prized possessions, if you're lucky enough to have survived the 10- or 15-year waiting list, are your season tickets. I am lucky enough to have four of those tickets.

So while Mike tried to calm me, on a hot night in June, and while I tried to stop crying, all I could think of was the opening home game coming up in September and would I be able to be there. Nothing else seemed to matter at that moment. Obviously my brain was not working again. I had heard about chemo-brain, but how could it be happening before chemo???

Mike tried to speak and I wailed, "But I have season tickets!"

At that point Mike probably thought that I had been transported to the wrong lab and that I should be having a brain scan since I obviously was deranged. The opening football game was my priority when looking death in the face—or so I thought.

He looked at me and said, "You'll be there, you'll be walking up those steps to your seat. You have one of the best doctors anywhere and you're going to be fine."

Now, he didn't know what might happen to me during the next week but he gave me hope. It gave me a real goal.

During the next few months I can't tell you how many times I held on to what he said.

Make goals for yourself during this ordeal. Don't make large ones. I couldn't concentrate on a book, nor could I do my stitching. Don't try anything to strain your brain. You're not going to learn Mandarin Chinese in a week, but maybe you could do a cross-word puzzle that had the word "Chinese" in it.

One of the first things I had done after I was released from the hospital, and could walk semi-comfortably, was a pedicure. That was a small goal that made me feel wonderful. At my next appointment the PAs saw my purple toenails and thought they looked great!!

I did get to that football game. I was having chemo treatments at the time and I was very tired but there I was, scarf on my hairless head and suntan lotion everywhere else. I did walk up those steps to my seat—just as Mike said I would.

Let's Do It

I was now back to the starvation therapy. No food yesterday, drink the liquids for the colonoscopy, no food. I figured it was a bit late to hope that this was going to starve that 25-pound tumor, but hope does spring eternal.

Now there still was no food. Not much to do but watch the television and watch the clock at the same time.

This must be how it feels when a prisoner is waiting to walk down the hall to the execution. I didn't know what to expect but I was sure that it was not going to be fun nor was it going to be a walk in the park. The longer I watched the clock the more panic stricken I was starting to feel. Not that I would let anyone know that. My husband didn't need the stress of knowing that he couldn't make things better, and Kathy would just say, "Everything's going to be fine."

... A TIME SCHEDULE RARELY IS FOLLOWED.

One of the things that you learn in a hospital is that a time schedule rarely is followed. Today was to be surgery day, but when exactly would this journey begin? No one could give me a time so there was no way that I could see the light at the end of the tunnel. Just relax, (were they kidding?), and things will unfold as planned. The problem was who was in charge of this plan? Certainly not I.

Everyone who knows me knows that I live by a tight time schedule and a timeline that stretches into the next season, if not year. I plan vacations a year in advance; obviously that didn't work for this year. All trips had to be postponed and rescheduled for a future time—if I made it through this. I always had a list in my hand or purse, things to buy, places to go, errands to run. My husband often joked that when I died I would probably have a list to hand God if I got to heaven.

So, when I was placed in a position where no one seemed to have a time line, although I am sure they did, they just didn't want to share it with me, I felt adrift. Just what was going to happen? And when?

The doctor had gone over all of the terrible things he may find during surgery, that should have given me plenty of things about which to worry. I did. At least I worried about those things he mentioned that I understood. But then I thought, worrying isn't going to change anything nor improve anything. Might as well take another nap.

Lunch time came and went-of course, no food.

The afternoon wore on, and on, and on.

The nurses kept coming in to see how I was doing, but they never revealed the rather vague time line by which we were being governed. I started to think that perhaps the delay is to subdue the patient, but more realistically the doctor is giving another patient all of the care that he later will give you. So you wait your turn and hope that your surgeon isn't overly tired when he does get to you.

More hours passed.

When you're at this stage you really can't anticipate what may go on in the operating room because that implies that you know what is going to happen. And you don't. So you're in this type of Neverland, not knowing what to think or what might happen. I had seen surgeries on TV, who hadn't, and I really didn't want to think of those.

And just when I thought, okay, they really did make a mistake and soon someone is going to come in here and tell me that this surgery had been cancelled because this young doctor had erred in his diagnosis. He would come in and apologize and I could then return home.

How wrong could I keep being?

Finally the transportation person and the nurse arrived in the room to move me to what I call the "holding tank" for surgery. I was the airplane being put into the holding flight pattern. The problem was where was this plane going and in what condition would it land?

Off I went. Nurses saying "good luck" (this must be really bad if they're wishing me good luck) and that they would be here when I returned.

The trip seemed to take forever. The hospital hallways covered miles and it seemed like we would never reach our destination.

I was placed in a cubicle, a woman stayed with me and asked questions. I noticed that they always have to ask questions. The problem here was that this woman had bathed in a tub full of the worst cologne that I have ever smelled. So here I was, in this small area, trying not to throw up from this very unpleasant scent. She kept talking and asked who my doctor was. When I told her she immediately went into her opinions of, not his skill or reputation, but how his behind looked in his scrubs! I would have found this rather amusing at another time, but this was not it.

My husband, Kathy and her pregnant daughter Rachel all were there. Rachel had been waiting to take a picture of the doctor, but every time she thought she had a chance she got involved in what he was saying to me and the photo never got taken. Months later we laughed about this, but at the time not much was funny.

We waited and waited, but we weren't ever told what was taking so long to get started. That's another hospital rule I guess. No one ever gives you answers.

Finally, there he was, Doctor- looks- good- in- scrubs. However, there were no scrubs, just regular everyday street clothes. No use asking him to turn around.

He came in, asked how I was doing, told me things were going to be all right, and said to give him a few minutes to get things ready. He looked at me and said, "Are you ready?" With those ever-present tears in my eyes I nodded "yes". I just couldn't get the words out. He said, "Okay, let's do it."

Kathy, George and Rachel kissed me. I made Kathy promise to take care of George if I were to die during surgery. George had made her promise the same thing when he had his heart attack. It looked like she kept getting the worst end of all of these ordeals. She assured me that she wouldn't have to take care of him because I would be back to them in a few hours. Another one of those comments backed up by no facts.

And then the real journey began. I was rolled down the hallway toward the doors that would lead me into the great, white, unknown, Dante's levels of hell came into my mind but at what level would I awaken?

So what's it really like in the OR? Basically, gray. Stainless steel does not come in colors, at least not in these rooms. A rather non-descript, light(easy on the eyes) green-walled environment. Some of these OR's are big, some small. They will have different types of equipment in them, depending on what type of surgery may be scheduled in that room.

When you're the one being wheeled to the OR you have no idea that you are going down a rather long hallway with rooms on either side-some larger than others. In some hospitals there could be as many as 12 or more in use at the same time. Chaos, you would think, but you, like I so often was, would be incorrect. To do the types of procedures with so few errors and mistakes in these places can be amazing—maybe that is why they always are behind—the nurses and doctors double check all of the patients and paperwork to minimize any error—not like on television where the delay is caused by the doctor and a nurse having sex in the on-call room. That scenario makes for good program ratings but not for good medicine.

If you have never been "backstage" and have only been "front and center" as the patient, then you have missed the most organized network of doctors, nurses, technicians and equipment imaginable. It puts Disneyworld to shame.

Each OR is equipped with instruments (two of each for the particular surgery), machinery and walls of supplies. The people who work in these approximate 500 square-foot rooms (now if you're trying to picture 500 square feet think of a two-car garage—much larger than they seem on Grey's Anatomy) can quickly locate anything on the shelves. I would need a pack of notecards and a chart to locate a specific item in that myriad of cubicles—taking more time than the surgery itself.

The rooms are kept at approximately 68 degrees for the comfort of the medical staff. You, the patient, need not fear being too cold-you are wrapped in layers of that blue paper sheeting. A surgery may take 2-4-6 hours or more, so the doctors need to be comfortable.

The lights are bright, the stainless steel glistening, similar to a car dealer showroom or, not a pleasant thought, a butcher shop!

As I have learned more and more about the medical profession, I am amazed at the misconceptions probably all of us have concerning our surgeons. There are plenty of jokes about how much money doctors make and how few hours they work. We often think of physicians as people who golf too much, take too many days off and only give us a limited amount of time when we see them in their offices. I would like to clear the air on these types of opinions right here. If you could be an observer in the OR as I was, you would quickly put those attitudes to bed.

HOW THEY SURVIVE THESE SCHEDULES IS ONE MORE MYSTERY IN LIFE.

These surgeons work morning to night on some days. Of course your urban doctors are much busier than perhaps doctors in a smaller area. Holidays, weekends, none are exempt. Patients have to be checked on and surgeries need to be done, nothing works on a 9-to-5 work schedule. In the 17th and 18th centuries this type of seven days a week, dawn–til–dark work schedule was considered a form of slavery. In the early 20th century unions gained footage to protect workers from unfair labor practices. What about the surgeon's hours? Add in possible research time and teaching young residents and you now have used more than the allotted 24 hours in a day! How they survive these schedules is one more mystery in life.

So here you are, waiting at the door to that mysterious room. It's really not that strange but you will never know because of course, you are asleep. So let me tell you what you may have missed.

While you are waiting in the hallway the room is getting prepared. When you get there the "staging" is ready. The equipment is in place, the instruments are lined up, the players are blue-gowned and ready to perform—just like a dramatic production. The difference is that a drama, or a Broadway musical, is not truly real. It is a representation of an event in the real or imaginary world. This, the OR, is real.

All of the "staging" is ready. If we look at this as a drama the problem might be, who is the "star"? Is it the patient, who is on the table, covered in blue sheeting but unaware of her position (rather embarrassing, no wonder they don't let us know these things) or is it the surgeon who is the main player and who will direct the others?

Unlike what we see on television, there was no idle chit-chat going on in the OR, at least not when I was there. I tend to believe that my doctor would not put up with a lot of unnecessary chatter while he and the team are working. After the observation we joked that no one was talking about who was sleeping with whom—as they often do on television. My husbands' first question was, "Were they talking about who got laid last night?" Needless to say, the answer was "no".

The Surgical Scrub Technician was at his table with an array of instruments-he knew where each was, again, how does he remember each piece of equipment? They all seem to look the same to me. As the surgeon asked for a specific item, it was placed in his hand. A constant "please" and "thank-you" could be heard throughout the procedure. Again, I am amazed at the level of politeness through my entire journey, even in the OR.

The nurse would leave the room to get anything that was needed but was not in the room. She labeled specimens, counted items used and noted on a chart which items were chargeable to the patient. She made sure that things were picked-up and that the area in use was free from any obstacles. She had to document and record many things that were occurring and that needed to be done so everything would go correctly.

When everything is just as it needs to be, the surgeon takes over.

As with all things in life, you have to be ready to change plans quickly. You, the patient, may think that you are going to have laproscopic surgery but the surgeon may find that he needs to cancel that idea and shift to regular surgery. Don't be surprised if you wake up later that day with a large incision!

The actual surgical opening is not very large. As I look at the long scar on my body I wondered why my opening had to be so large. When I later asked about this I was jokingly told that my surgeon had been looking for that "25-pound turkey"!!

Four hands, the doctor and the PA, and equipment all are focused in this small opening. It reminds you of stuffing a turkey! The most surprising part of this surgery to me was that there was not a lot of blood flying all over the place. In fact, there was very little. Your incision site is constantly being wiped out with cloths, towels, and the cauterization process is frequently happening. Your abdominal area is constantly being pulled and pushed—thus the reason for being so bruised after a surgery. There is a piece of equipment attached to the body to keep the incision open (an abdominal retractor) similar to the device attached to your mouth when the dentist fills a tooth.

So let's look at this as a Broadway production.

The stage is set—all of the actors are in place and the main character enters, hands dripping. He quickly is handed the other parts of his "costume," his gloves and a blue gown to wear over his scrubs. Now everyone is in place.

The well-choreographed "dance" begins. Every person knows where their "mark" is on this stage and no one has a mis-step, no one gets in any other person's way or field of vision. "Props" are asked for, they are received and used and then returned to the "prop manager"-the Surgical Scrub Nurse and the OR nurse. Without the "props" there would be no story, no surgery.

As with a production where you are advised to "please turn off all cell phones and recording devices" prior to a surgery, the surgical team stops and the surgeon states the patients' name, type of procedure and other important information to ensure that everyone in the room is in agreement that the correct surgery is being performed on the correct patient. As in a play, everyone has the correct script and knows just what to do.

The surgeon and his PA move in unison. They know each step. And when the time is right these two raise their arms above the "field" and announce that they are going to switch sides, then they move to opposite sides of the patient. The dance continues.

At one point the surgeon appears to need more light. The nurse helps to adjust the lights, all is well. No lighting director here, this is a do-it-yourself process in this production.

As the production moves on the nurse changes her gloves many times. The "costumes" do not stay the same, just like in a play. The surgeon calls for a clean robe. The production continues for 2 1/2 hours with no intermission and no coffee breaks. The stamina that these professionals have is amazing. They don't seem to tire, their hands don't drop anything and they are focused and calm.

No one takes the patient for granted. They do their job to the best of their abilities. They are not there to win awards, or to get bonuses, they are there to save lives no matter how long it takes, or how much their legs, hands and backs ache. They may have planned on a ballgame in the evening but if the surgery takes longer than expected then the team will have to win on its own—even if their child plays on that team. They do give up a lot of life for others.

SUSAN EVANS

62

As I watched this production I marveled at the wonders of science and the knowledge that these physicians and their teams have. No one needed to check a fact, read a direction, or look at a computer for help. How many people have jobs that demand that much memory and skill? Most of us can rely on outside information at a moment's notice to get a job done. We may have skills in our particular areas, but I doubt that they are honed to this degree.

As the surgery neared a close, I was entranced by the stitching and stapling. How many hours did it take to learn to be this precise with those stitches? I am a stitcher who is constantly "inventing" a new stitch when I make a mistake or count my pattern incorrectly. Not here. The neatest little row of stitches appeared on the patient and then a line of tiny staples. (I wonder if they can mend a tear or hem a skirt?)

As the production winds down, the props need to be accounted for. The OR nurse begins the count. The system is methodical and everything is where it should be. The "show" is over, the production a success and the players complete their work.

After I had witnessed this amazing procedure I thought back to a conversation that I had had with my doctor at the very beginning of this project. I had once asked him if he ever got "rusty" when he did not get to do a lot of surgeries. He answered me by saying, "No, I'm very good at what I do."

That made me wonder if this project, with this ego, was going to be no walk in the park. Now that I had observed a surgery I understood why this type of self-confidence is necessary. It is not arrogance. Rather, it is the assurance that as a doctor he (and others) knows what to do. Far better than getting the answer, "Well, maybe I could be rusty, I don't know, I'm not really sure how it would affect my performance." No one wants a doctor who lacks confidence in his skills.

As I left the OR my only thought was "Holy Jesus!" I had just seen an amazing procedure, maybe not exactly a miracle, but it certainly would seem a miracle when anyone survives this type of bodily intrusion. The next time you see your physician or surgeon, thank him or her. They get a lot of criticism and probably not a lot of thanks.

SUSAN EVANS

Interrupted "Lesson Plan"

It, whatever "it" was, was over. I felt myself being rolled into a room, and I opened my eyes to see my husband, Kathy and her daughter Rachel all smiling and giving me the thumbs-up sign.

That was very reassuring, but my primary concern at that moment was this awful feeling of a full bladder and the urgent need to pee. Again, never having any experience with any type of surgery I was sure that I did not like this feeling. The nurse immediately told me that the feeling was normal because I had a Foley catheter and that is how it worked. There's that vocabulary again—what is a Foley catheter? And why don't these people give more information so that we don't have to figure out how to pose a semi-intelligent question right after coming out of anesthesia?

I learned that medically this catheter is a handy device that helps to drain the bladder and hopefully keep the patient more comfortable. During a major surgery the bladder muscle may stretch and this could cause pain; also, our bodies will have difficulty peeing and the bladder will just fill. Not a very pleasant thought. Also, these medical professionals do not want the patient trying to get out of bed to use the bathroom before it is safe to do so. Fine, but the constant pumping feeling was a bit annoying.

I was deposited back in my room, everyone kissed me good night—I wondered what time it was and how long the surgery had taken, I later found out that it had taken about four hours, which was considered normal—and off they went. Thankfully, at this point I slept. Had the doctor stopped in to check on me? Who knows, I surely didn't. I am sure those demons were right outside of my door, but for this night I didn't care.

The next day dawned and I was still alive so I thought things must have gone fairly well. I hadn't seen any angels, my parents were not by my side and I could see Oakland outside of my huge window. The sun was streaming through the glass, the day looked beautiful and I was on a new part of this journey.

AT LEAST IN PRISON YOU GOT WATER!

However, this cursed Foley catheter was still in operation. I was not allowed out of bed and there was still no food or even water. At least in prison you got water!

I missed most of that day, sleeping and saying a few words to my husband and friend filled the time and then it was dark. I was so used to the techs coming in to take blood that when they did I hardly woke up–I just stuck my arm out from under the sheet and dozed off while they did their work. The bad part is that right about this time the anesthesia had worn off and I was much more aware of that catheter! By about this time I felt that if the doctors did not cause pain and discomfort they would feel that they had shortchanged me on my surgery. They all were starting to look a bit diabolical to me.

For the most part I was comfortable and I did not feel pain, only discomfort. I was swaddled in this tight elastic-like Velcro "binder" and felt very comfortable and cozy. It obviously was doing a good job of keeping any discomfort to a minimum.

The members of the "flock" would visit each morning, open the binder, check the incision, swaddle me again and tell me that everything was fine. Nothing wrong with this, except the catheter was still operating.

I felt like the character in Poe's *The Tell-Tale Heart*. Instead of thinking the heart was beating loud enough for everyone to hear, I was plagued with the constant draining and pressure from that sadistic Foley. I still am pretty sure that it must have been designed during the Spanish Inquisition.

And that's when I turned from a cooperative patient to one who wasn't so cooperative. It was bound to happen. I had been nice for a much longer period of time than my friends and my husband ever thought was possible in this situation.

At 4 the next morning I grabbed my cell phone, called my husband and announced to him that I was going to refuse treatment. It was my right and I was going to exert it. That got him leaping out of bed and grabbing the car keys to get to the hospital before they did throw me out. I knew I had plenty of time to get what I wanted done before he could drive across town and talk me out of my, what he thought was, a misguided plan. The morning city traffic would keep him away just long enough.

In came the flock. They examined the sutures—again everything was going as planned.

Wrong—they just didn't know it yet.

I asked that the catheter be removed. The answer was that it couldn't be removed yet. They realized it was uncomfortable but it had to do its job and that job wasn't quite finished yet.

At that point I was out of patience.

"Ladies," I said. "I have the right to refuse treatment and that is what I am doing right now. Remove the catheter."

I wanted to add a few adjectives that I thought would be more forceful but I restrained myself and did try to exude some type of maturity and professionalism.

Again they tried to dissuade me. Again I repeated myself. "I have the right to refuse treatment and that is what I am doing." At this point they were probably thinking, "Who is going to do the paperwork for the refusal of treatment?"

As the group looked upon what they probably thought was a long day coming up, one slipped out the door and before I could blink, there was the doctor. What do these doctors do, lurk outside the door just so they can jump in when needed?

He sat down, and I could tell by his tone of voice that he was more than annoyed. On top of that I imagined that he had probably been up all night, you can tell when people don't enjoy enough sleep, and these people seemed to never sleep. The flock had quietly left the room, they probably didn't want to be witnesses to me throwing something at that point, or they may have gone for security, who knows?

So the doctor began, in a rather angry tone, that he did not want his staff abused and he thought that perhaps I had verbally abused them. I assured him, in an equally annoyed tone (mine was probably better, I was older and had more experience at being pissed off at people) that I had been very polite and that I had not abused his staff. He did agree that they had not told him that I had been nasty. I guess he just assumed that.

He went through the same points that they had. This was a very bad decision, it could cause unnecessary pain, blah, blah, blah. He then referred to his sister who was a teacher and said that when she has a lesson plan it is followed to accomplish all of the points in the lesson which she is teaching. Did he think I didn't know about lesson plans? I had written them for 32 years! Six different classes a day, five days a week for 32 years. You do the math.

He referred to "his" lesson plan, the Foley catheter. I heard what he had to say but that didn't mean I listened. Every teacher knows the difference between listening and hearing.

I knew he was right, he had my best interest at hand, but I couldn't stand that catheter one more minute.

He got up from the couch, it reminded me of my father when I had pestered him enough to get my way—not hard for an only child and a girl at that—and he knew he had lost the argument. This wasn't a "who-would-win" competition. This was my life I was dealing with, but still, I wanted that awful catheter out.

"It's your choice," he said, "but I do not recommend it." I already knew that, didn't I?

The catheter was removed in one quick motion and I felt relieved, even though I did feel badly that I had to play my trump card, but sometimes you just have to do what you have to do and the devil be damned.

I now rested comfortably, could get out of bed and even walked a little.

Halfway through the day, there he was, the doctor, coming through the door. I suppose he was coming in to check if I had died from my poor decision. Instead he found me up and comfortable and in a much better frame of mind. Again, he told me what problems could have occurred from my poor, obstinate decision. I was polite, told him I understood, but that I felt fine.

He tried to refrain from smiling, but one was creeping on his face, and he said, "Well, I guess you know your own body."

Point made!

And the real point of this was my "medical rights" assertion. Sometimes there is a fire drill, or a bomb scare and your lesson plan goes out the window. At least in the non-medical world it does.

"Check-Out" Time

As with all journeys, sooner or later the trip comes to an end, or in this case, what seemed like an end. It was time to "check-out" of this medical cocoon that had kept me safe and warm for all of these days. This wasn't unlike leaving a hotel: collect your belongings, get ready for the "real" world, say good-bye to the new people you have met, and find something to wear home!

After my surgery that had taken place on Monday, the doctor had hoped that I could leave on Thursday. Those few days were filled with physical therapists walking me up and down the halls and helping me to negotiate stairs. I seemed to have no problems with these tasks but I wasn't quite convinced that Thursday would be check-out time from my medical five-star hotel.

It wasn't.

I heard the words, "Hun, I think you need to stay a few more days." Now before we continue let me explain the "hun" part. For those of you who are not from Pittsburgh, you may not realize that we Pittsburghers have a unique vocabulary, and a sound, all of our own. "Hun" as in "honey" is not a sexist, politically incorrect word. It is something we all say. It is a friendly term. When someone says "hun" to us we feel like we're all part of one big family. That's just another thing that makes this city so special.

A few more days incarcerated would do the trick.

Now here's another point to be made. If you're not strong enough, or don't feel ready to go it alone, say so. Of course your insurance coverage probably will have something to say about this, but I'm sure those hospitals know more than a few ways to get around that problem.

Another problem I had that no one seemed to be addressing—and we were running out of question time if I was to be released from this place—was this rubber thing sticking out of my belly. What was this thing?

When you go into surgery no one tells you that you're coming out with a rubber balloon-like mechanism protruding from your incision site. Periodically an aide would drain the balloon—not a pleasant feeling. Who was going to do this once I got home? (Who do you think??)

Saturday dawned and I was given the hope that a quick exit might be on the horizon. (Did you notice the "quick" in what I said? Obviously I am a slow learner.)

This is where I think another procedure needs reevaluated. After all of the physical and emotional trauma associated with cancer surgery, where is the **real** doctor? Sure it was a Saturday, yes they have a life too, but at that moment in the hospital I would think that my life would be important enough to warrant five minutes from my doctor. Maybe he/she has 10 patients being discharged that day—give them each 10 minutes or less, that's not even two hours. The patient would feel more secure and the doctor could go off feeling good that this selfless conduct helped someone. Off he/she could go to shoot 18 holes, do some research, have some family time, or whatever it is they do on their own time.

As a high school teacher, no one had more papers to correct than an English teacher. I gave up many Fridays and Saturdays correcting those papers. There were innumerable days in those 32 years that began at 5:30a.m and didn't end until 2 or 3 in the morning. Unpaid time.

Of course I realize that saving lives is more important than correcting a senior high school research paper on Shakespeare when the student doesn't care if you mean William Shakespeare or Shakespeare fishing rods.

However, the exit interview was done by a resident, or a fellow, or someone a pay grade well below the top of the scale. In my case, a young man came in, checked everything and told me that yes, indeed, I would be leaving today.

Wonderful! And then I asked obviously the wrong question. "What time do you think I'll be going?" This seemed like a logical question to me. After all, my husband had to pick me up. This wasn't a situation where I was going to wait for a bus or hail a cab.

This young doctor looked at me with a rather irritated expression (they all need much more sleep) and said, "This isn't a hotel you know. When we're ready you'll go."

Notice he said "we're" and not "you're".

So once again, paperwork, protocol, rules and regulations come before patient satisfaction. I must admit this was one of the few times that a doctor was semi-rude to me, and I'll chalk it up to cultural differences (not all cultures deal with women the same way).

I waited a few more hours, wondering if I should call the city newsroom and have them cover my leaving the hospital at some point that day dressed only in a hospital gown and my flip-flops. Probably not a good picture.

The hours wore on and in came that same doctor-he would never last at the check-out desk at the Plaza. He announced that he was going to remove that "drain"—previously I had been told that I would go home with it attached to me and that I would have to drain it and then return to have it removed at a later date.

THEY NEVER TELL YOU THE TRUTH ABOUT PAIN.

I asked him if this would hurt—why did I keep asking that foolish question? They never tell you the truth about pain.

He started to tug at the tube—yes it hurt—I grabbed his white-coated right arm and hung on for my life (or so it seemed). I suppose that forced him to work with his left. He did, it was out, it hurt, but I was not dead! One step closer to "check-out" time.

SUSAN EVANS

All of my belongings, including all of the beautiful flowers, had been removed from my room the night before. The nurses came in with a multitude of directions, the aides tried to get my flip-flops on—you're never told how much your feet will swell in the hospital—and papers were signed. Getting a passport to leave this country does not require as much paperwork as trying to get out of a hospital.

Finally, transportation was summoned.

It was time to roll down those halls hopefully for the last time and to finally breathe fresh air and feel the sun. I was leaving this medical safety zone that had saved my life and kept me "warm and fuzzy" for so many days.

As with all trips there's a feeling of nostalgia. I had met some wonderful people who had made my journey as comfortable as possible. I had learned a lot, not just medically, but about my own strength and I had beaten those demons several times.

Now it was time to try it somewhat on my own.

As I was rolled to the front doors I thought that the journey was over. I had checked out, I was awaiting transportation—what else could happen?

Here we go, out of the wheelchair and into our SUV, are they kidding??? How was I to get from ground level to seat level? I did not see a crane or a lift to help with his job. The aide helped me to stand on my own and between the two of us I got into that seat that had never seemed as high as it did that day. And then the seatbelt! My stomach was distended from the surgery, I would have thought that once the 25-pound turkey was removed that I would look quite thin, not so. This was not going to work. And it didn't. Sometimes you just have to do what you have to do and a bad idea is often the only one that works. So it was no seatbelt.

I mentally was defying a policeman to stop this car and ask why I didn't have the seatbelt fastened. All of those George Carlin words were getting polished in my mind, I was ready to give a rather colorful explanation if need be. Thankfully,

I MENTALLY WAS DEFYING A POLICEMAN TO STOP THIS CAR...

SUSAN EVANS

none of my mental explanation was necessary and we arrived safely back at the condo.

I had mastered the SUV but what about the 12 steps up to our door? The flip-flops were barely on, I was weak, and those steps looked higher than when I had last seen them, but up I went. My husband stayed behind me in case I fell. I grabbed the railings and got to the door to be greeted by our dog.

Home at last!

And Then The Dog Ran Away

Finally I could travel the three hours to return to our primary home—not a pleasant trip when the stents made you have to pee every 45 minutes and when there were few restrooms between there and here. But I made it.

Home in my own bed, get some strength so I could return to Pittsburgh and start the chemotherapy. At least I could be up and walk and face the next crisis in my ever—crisis—filled summer.

While I was in the hospital the entire sewer system at home, three and a half hours away, had backed up which required immediate repair. The neighbors jumped in and took care of everything, even washing all of the wet towels used to clean up the laundry room. Crisis averted. Right? Wrong again.

By the time I returned home, I thought things were back to normal. Not so. More sewer problems. Now the backhoe was ripping up the driveway and part of the garage floor, and the plumber was finding even more problems. No resting here; the noise level never lessened and our Sheltie, "Regan," was on the verge of a nervous breakdown.

So what do you do when all of this is at your door? Escape. What else!

My friend Kathy—more like the sister I never had— arrived at the destruction site and whisked me off to breakfast. What a pleasure to enjoy no noise and someone who understood why I was still crying every five minutes.

We returned home, opened the door and immediately noticed that no furry friend greeted us. Our minds both flew to a while back when the dog had run away and wasn't found for 18 long, terrifying hours. (If you're not a dog lover, then you may not be able to relate to the angst which we felt at this moment.)

So where was the dog? My husband and all of the workers swore that no one had opened a door. Now this dog is smart but she's not quite tall enough to reach the door handle on her own!

Everyone stopped their work and searched. No luck.

Living in a small town does afford the modicum of caring people who know you. Within hours, people all over the community were searching for this animal. No luck.

Days went by, thunderstorms (she is deathly afraid of thunder and rain) hot weather, coyotes in the woods, not to mention bear. No dog.

Weeks went by. I had another appointment at Magee with Dr. Jaffee who assured me that the dog would come home. Nice guy that Jaffee, but what did he know about my dog?

Every once in a while people would call and say they saw the dog in the woods, or near a local resort, but no one could catch her. She wouldn't go to strangers.

My husband and friend Kathy scoured the hillsides, the woods, and the various sections of town we never knew existed. No dog.

Days, weeks, a month went past. By this time I was doing the chemotherapy and wishing that I could have that dog here

SUSAN EVANS

to comfort me. Just to see her little head peek over the bed would have been a great help. No such luck.

Finally my husband and I and our friends all resigned ourselves to the fact that the dog was dead and that we had to move on. The tears were there again and I started to wonder how much one woman actually could cry. Do we have an unlimited amount of tears or was I almost to my end?

I AM GOING TO GO BACK AND TRAP HER.

Sixty-seven days later the phone rang and a man we didn't know called and said, "I saw your dog and I am going to go back and trap her." Within an hour the man was back on the phone asking directions to our home so that he could deliver this poor lost dog. We were so excited but skeptical, of course.

We called our friends, and Kathy came running over-there she was, so excited that she had put her clothes on inside out!! After we got her back in order we went to the corner of our street to wait for the wonderful people who said they had found the dog. We waited, and waited, and waited—you know how it is when you are expecting to see someone and it takes longer than you think it should. As we waited Steve, Kathy's husband, started to prepare the back of his SUV for the arrival of what would probably be a very dirty dog.

Finally a red truck pulled up with a cage in the back. By this time many of the neighbors had congregated at the bottom of the hill to welcome our "Regan" back home.

But was this our dog? Covered in mud, almost skeletal, and smelling very badly. Was this the princess who never got her feet dirty and expected her dinner at exactly 4:30 every day?

It sure was. She looked at us with sad eyes and we all looked at her with tears in ours.

After a long scrubbing, she ate and went to sleep as if nothing had ever happened. She looked at us as if to say, "what's the big deal?"

Now, one of the remarkable parts of this story is that the dog was found at the beginning of October, the week honoring St. Francis, the patron saint of animals. God does work in various ways.

The timing was perfect.

So when I was going through the roughest part of my chemo, there was that little furry head peeking over my bed and making me smile even though I felt like I wasn't going to see the next day.

The dog was home. St. Francis had taken care of that, and Dr. Jaffee was right. The obvious moral: Trust your urologist.

SUSAN EVANS

Working Through The Steps

Once you hear your doctor tell you the diagnosis and once you have asked as many questions as your numb mind can ask, you move as if in a fog for a while. What's going to happen next? How will I continue my life? Who will help me? All of a sudden it starts to sound like someone died instead of someone who is going to live.

We are all familiar with the Seven Stages of Grief—we have seen people try to work through those stages when they lose a loved one, and we even may have tried to help them work through the stages. The stages usually don't follow the progression as listed in a textbook; life rarely does. Sometimes several stages merge into one, sometimes one stage reappears more than once, but when it's all said and done those stages, when recognized and accepted, may help you through this cancer diagnosis. Putting emotions "in order" often helps in accepting those emotions and in building on them to help us see the light at the end of the tunnel. But emotions are not textbook.

Let's start with **SHOCK AND DENIAL**

I was home from the hospital for a few days when the phone call came. My doctor had called to tell me that the pathology report had indeed shown cancer, Stage 3. Could I even breathe as I held the phone? Not likely, although all I could hear was Stage 3, one stage away from the worst stage.

He assured me that it wasn't as bad as I thought. He explained that there were three stages of Stage 3; A, B, and C and I had Stage 3-A, a good survival rate. But he would like me to begin my chemotherapy as soon as possible. That didn't sound too good to me. Remember, the stents were still in and I couldn't sit for more than 45 minutes without running to the bathroom. How was I going to sit for three hours during chemo?

FIVE YEARS!!

I asked, "After the six treatments were completed, then would I be cured"?

"We can't say you're cured for five years," my doctor answered. Five years!! This just can't be.

At this point, and for this conversation, I would have much rather been in his office and had him tell me in person. At a time like this I think the personal touch may be more important than a doctor's schedule, but at least it wasn't an e-mail! Looking back I think that sometimes a doctor really cares about a patient and would rather not relate bad news face-to-face. I would like to suggest that if this is the case the doctor needs to realize that if he expects the patient to accept the diagnosis then he should be able to accept it also. I know. Time schedules.

I believe that in my case he was trying to save me a rather uncomfortable ride across town to his office. He later explained to me that he thought calling the patient first and then scheduling a face-to-face is a good idea. That way the patient may have several days to think of questions. When you are first told of a cancer diagnosis it is hard to think of anything remotely important to ask. Like with everything else, this technique works with some and not with others. I would have liked face-to-face first.

Cancer, Stage 3, this just couldn't be. Not me. There's the denial jumping in. Shock goes right with it. Psychologically, shock provides emotional protection from being overwhelmed all at once. Right at this point I think I had hit emotional bankruptcy.

PAIN AND GUILT

There was no physical pain. There were no symptoms. A swollen ankle was the only sign I had. But there is pain of the heart, not heart attack pain, just a sadness that this is happening to you. Remember, don't ask, "Why me?"

Guilt rides in next.

During this time I had a person imply that perhaps this was God's way of punishing me since I had never had children. Now there's some guilt to think about, for maybe a second, because that type of foolish, mean-spirited comment does not deem any extra thought. You are going to run into people, even doctors, who will relish putting the blame on you. The "Maybe-if-you-would- have-listened-to-me-this-wouldn't-have-happened" comment from a physician was totally unnecessary and on the verge of unprofessional. Steel yourself to ignore all of these types of remarks, concentrate on the positive. Remember, don't let your attitude control you, you control it.

As I sat in my doctor's waiting room one day, I noticed a woman with very short hair. We began to speak and she told me how she had had hair that was very long, she had never cut it in her life. Now she would not have enough time to grow it back. She went on to mention that she was an elementary school teacher and since she had contracted cancer her problems at work were with her colleagues. They gave her a very hard time, while her students were kind and understanding. It's going to happen. Sometimes adults are not so adult.

What could I have done to prevent this? I previously had had a test for blood clots, negative. I had had the blood test for ovarian cancer, the C125 test, again, negative. I later found out that this test was not fool-proof. According to the *Pittsburgh Post-Gazette,* May 5, 2013, this test for ovarian cancer was one of the eight cancer screenings to avoid because the screenings are not very effective.

Again, forget the "Why Me?" Should I have gone to the doctor more often? (Perhaps if I could find one that I liked I would have) but nonetheless I was just overridden with a feeling of guilt but with no apparent reason. Isn't it funny how the mind works?

Now that you have somewhat overcome the feelings of grief, shock and guilt, the real emotions jump in: **ANGER AND BARGAINING.**

Of course I was angry. I had never really been sick in my life. I didn't even get flu shots and rarely did I get the flu. Working in a high school leaves you open for every germ imaginable, but I still didn't get ill very often. So what was this all about? I couldn't have cancer, I was too busy, too many community obligations. At this point in my life I was president of our local Rotary and had to be at the end of the year dinner with my "goodbye" speech. I couldn't be in a hospital. Couldn't this just wait a few weeks? My husband and I had our annual trip planned to Hilton Head. Couldn't this then wait a month or two, what about until after September? No amount of bargaining was going to make this palatable—it was what it was. I could be as angry as I wanted to be, it was still there. Now I knew what the Hebrew saying, *"A mentsh tracht un"* ("Man plans, God laughs") means.

Anger rarely does much except let us vent our emotions. I was angry only for a short time. Angry at whom? For what reason? What good would it do? All of these thoughts ran through my head and of course all pointed to the fact that anger was a waste of time.

My doctor told me that he felt that anger and blame are a huge waste of time. They change your focus. As a cancer patient you should focus on healing from the surgery, having a healthy lifestyle to help get you through the treatments and a positive outlook so that you can beat anything. Mind, body and soul—all are just as important as chemotherapy to get the best outcome for the patient. All of those positive forces were things I felt that I could control.

With whom was I going to bargain? I tried bargaining with my primary care physician the first day in the local hospital. Couldn't I go home and have my husband drive me to the hospital in Pittsburgh? Absolutely not. The blood clots could move and I could die. Couldn't I go home for a few days and get my life in order? Same answer. No amount of bargaining would change anything.

So, the type A personality, the only child syndrome kicks in—I couldn't have my way, not something I was very used to. Sometimes the situation did look like it was going from bad to worse.

DEPRESSION, REFLECTION, LONELINESS

Now I could understand what the oxymoronic phrase (there's one of those vocabulary words that not everyone knows, it means: contradictory words; a phrase in which two words of contradictory meaning are used for special effect–a wise fool, a little giant) "in this together, by ourselves" really meant.

My friends were there to help my husband and me. They brought food constantly, called to make sure we were okay, sent loads of flowers, cards by the dozens, and prayed. I think every church in this small community had me on a prayer list. The support was there, but I was in this alone when I really thought about it.

Depression is foreign to me. The common definition of this term is "a mental disorder characterized by episodes of all-encompassing low mood accompanied by low self-esteem and loss of interest or pleasure in normally enjoyable activities." I was not depressed, I would have liked to resume my normal activities, or even have an interest in them, but I knew that in time I would be back doing what I liked to do. The more I was positive for my friends and husband the more I found myself thinking positively about myself.

When going through chemo Kathy would call at the beginning to see how I was doing and then she would say, "I'll catch you on the other side." Her youngest daughter had gone through a similar problem many years before and she knew what I was going through. After about five days, I would be on "the other side," so to speak, and would call her. I always knew she would be there when I felt well enough to talk.

There's a difference in my mind between loneliness and being lonely. I never felt totally alone because there always were friends, PAs, nurses, to give a hug or to wipe a tear. I never felt deserted in this suffering. I believe another reason that

I did not feel alone was that I prayed a lot during this time. When I was in the hospital I knew that a supreme being was watching over me and that my doctor was sent to make sure that I would survive this. Whatever it takes, do it.

Emotionally, things were looking a bit better by this time. The surgery was over. I had the diagnosis and the treatment schedule. Nothing left but to move on and trust everyone in charge. I certainly no longer was in charge. I was on the **UPWARD TURN.**

Now that I saw myself as more functional, not crying all of the time, my mind started to work again and I began to get into the three-week routine; drive to Pittsburgh, meet with the PA or the doctor, be examined and then go to chemo. Drive back home, drink a lot of liquids and get to bed before the queasy stomach started. Take the pills, sleep a lot and then start over. Just when I started to feel a bit normal it was back in the car and the three-week schedule began again. I was starting to mold my life in these three-week increments- I was **RESTRUCTURING AND WORKING THROUGH.**

And finally I was at the last step—**ACCEPTANCE AND HOPE.**

Chemo was moving along, and as much as I felt like I some-times couldn't go on, I did. A day would pass and I would feel a bit better, or I would call my wonderful chemo nurse,

Chris, and tell her the pills weren't working, a new prescription was tried and then I did feel better. My legs ached, another pill. I often joked that this definitely was better living through chemistry!

Obviously, there was a remedy for everything, except death.

I did have hope. Although my husband had to give me twice daily injections of Lovonox, and twice daily clean and pack part of my incision that had not closed properly, we could count the months and knew that these injections and packings would not be forever. There was hope and my medical staff was constantly there to assure me that things were moving along.

Through all of this, my husband was at my side. Each day when he had done all that he could to help me, and when he could think of nothing else to make me comfortable, he would sit by my bedside while I dosed in and out of sleep. The television would be on, I'm sure he wasn't interested in the programming, but he sat, and sat, and sat.

He was the strength that helped me through all of the days. Always with a positive outlook, even putting his work on hold and his life. He rarely got to his exercise program at the local hospital, and he often missed important meetings. He never complained. I sure could learn a lesson in patience from this man.

When I broke down in tears to my one PA, Nora, that I was getting nothing done at home, except a lot of sleeping, and that I felt frustrated, she said, "You are doing something…you are recovering from cancer surgery, that's your 'job' right now." She was right, but I was anxious to get back to normal.

I learned another valuable lesson: Slow down. Don't be in a hurry. Your life will fly by and you won't even be aware that it's going or nearly gone. Enjoy each moment. What gets done, gets done.

When You're Walking Through Hell, Just Keep Walking

I was home, resting and trying not to think of the next step—chemo. No one can fully realize the fear that that one word can instill in your mind and in your heart. What exactly is this stuff and what does it do? Are there any guarantees? How sick will I be? After it's over, will I be back to "normal?"

I soon would discover what Winston Churchill meant when he said, "When you're walking through hell, just keep walking."

The medical staff leads you through this section of your life. There is a chemo nurse assigned to you who goes over a giant binder full of information, using those words that the average person doesn't grasp. Unfortunately, my chemo nurse, Chris, was not in that day and I had someone I did not relate to very well. As she zipped through all of the pages that she felt were necessary, coughing the entire time, she told me to buy a bottle of B-6 vitamins, told me I would lose my hair within the week, suggested I buy a wig right away and gave me a list of places to shop for one, make sure I take the steroids the night before and the morning of, and lots of other information that I was not able to process at the time.

I was warned that the steroids would make me "jumpy" and that I probably would not sleep the night before a chemo treatment. Good. One more inconvenience on my road to recovery!

I left that office wondering how I was going to get through this. I asked for a tour of the chemo facility. It was late on a Friday afternoon, but since I was once again crying they felt sorry for me and agreed to take me through the facility.

As I was escorted past the massage chairs and personal televisions I once again thought that this place was indeed "spa-like." A lovely young nurse who saw me crying came running up to me to assure me that everything would be all right. She explained everything and went to her station and penciled me in on her work sheet for the following Monday.

She assigned herself to me, and I felt a bit better at least knowing someone in this area.

I chose to do all of my chemo treatments in Pittsburgh because I found it almost impossible to schedule them in my local hospital. Rural medicine cannot compare with urban medicine nor can the facilities that you must use. Our local hospital ran the chemo lab only two days a week, insisted that I have a port put in, and wanted to see all of the paperwork from Magee just in case the local doctor wanted to "change" something. Now, there was no way I was going to approve of their changing anything that my Pittsburgh doctor had ordered. That put the end to trying to "buy local" as the saying goes. All cancer care is not equal, even within a city, and that's why you need to select your facility and doctor carefully.

Again, remember, it's your life and you have the right to make the decisions. Do not be badgered by your local doctor if you feel that someone else is much better. Obviously, it was my opinion that my local hospital felt that its needs were more important than my needs. Never hesitate to get a second opinion. Don't worry if your doctor gets upset-that's not your problem. You need the best care that you can get, don't worry about someone else's feelings.

NEVER HESITATE TO GET A SECOND OPINION.

SUSAN EVANS

Monday dawned. Contrary to what I had been told, I had slept. I took the second dose of steroids and got into the car for the drive to the beginning of hell. As we crawled through the morning rush-hour traffic, my husband trying to stay calm, I screeched at him, "This is the second worst day of my life and I'm going to be late!" The traffic wasn't his fault and we had left home in plenty of time but he was taking the brunt of my fear that morning, and many more mornings to come.

We did arrive at the appointment on time and after being examined by Nora, one of the PAs in the doctor's office, I was sent upstairs for my first chemo treatment. If someone would have checked my pulse rate and blood pressure at that time, I am sure that the numbers would have been off the charts!

I received my wristband and sat with the other women who also were waiting for their names to be called. There's that feeling again—we may be in this together but we are alone. I sat and was afraid to look at anyone. No one else was on the verge of tears, perhaps they were veterans at this.

And then there was my nurse, Melana, waiting for me at the door. She walked with me to the area, got me comfortable in the chair, showed me all the controls, adjusted the television, told me she had prayed for me in her church on Sunday, explained what would happen and then she got down to the business at hand. Out came the needle and the IV tubes.

Now, some people were meant to be nurses and some were not. Thankfully, I got one who had all of the skills necessary to make me feel comfortable. I hardly felt the needle go into my vein, and she was so comforting that I started to think, "How bad can this be?"

I could watch television, have a massage in the chair and have my lunch delivered to me. Snacks were always available as were juices, soft drinks, and always comforting words. Again, it seemed like a fancy hotel spa had started to give chemo treatments. This is the way medicine should be and the way patients should be treated.

No matter how comfortable they tried to make this experience, three hours is a long time to sit, and I do not sit still very well. That was fine. Mel showed me how to unplug the IV machine and let it run on its battery and said I could walk anywhere I liked as long as I didn't get lost.

That made me feel less confined and I often did get up and take the machine with me.

Three hours is a long time for patient or spouse to sit, but there was my husband, always at my side. He would watch TV, work on his computer and even nap. His very presence made me feel stronger knowing that someone was there for me. It wasn't easy for him either and between the both of us I think we traveled a few miles just walking the halls.

Near the end of the treatment Mel came with papers to be signed, next appointment scheduled and a sheet advising me on what to do when I returned home. Drink lots of liquids for the first few days, (had they forgotten about the stents?), eat small meals, stay away from fried foods, (I guess that meant no McDonalds on the way home) rest, avoid aspirin, to name a few. She made sure I knew about the Compazine for the nausea and she suggested that if it didn't help to call the office and they would prescribe something else. (It didn't work and they prescribed Zofran, which was the life-saver of the experience.)

Off I went to our other home in Cranberry Township, feeling fine. I took a nap and started to wonder if this was how all the treatments would be. How foolish of me to think that.

The next day we drove the three and a half hours to our home in Northwestern Pennsylvania, stopping along the way all too often because of the stents. I still felt fine.

And then I didn't.

Off to bed. I tried to sleep, a constant feeling of car-sickness overtaking me. However, through this entire experience I did not vomit once. But those demons that I left in the hospital had found me. I fell into a routine: sleep, try to eat something, sleep, take a shower, sleep, try to eat, sleep. Then the body aches began. I had never felt pain in my legs like this. Take the Vicodine, sleep, eat, start over. Day after day. No energy, no ability to walk farther than the bathroom, no desire to do a thing, even the television did not provide any solace. There should be an FCC commission to improve television viewing during the daytime hours. I watched every house-selling, home improvement show that HGTV offered. I knew the prices for real estate in every corner of this country.

I knew I should eat, but what was it that I could eat? A piece of toast, a cracker, half a cookie, nothing substantial and nothing very healthy. Some days it was eggs (there goes the cholesterol) but my cardiologist assured me that everything would be fine in the end. The ginger ale was always at my bedside, and I ate more popsicles than a kindergarten class on a summer field trip.

My husband was there through all of this. He would sit by my bed at night while I tried to watch TV. He would prepare food which I wouldn't eat. He slept on a couch in the adjoining room so that he could hear me at night if I wanted something. There was nothing he didn't do to help me.

THERE WAS NOTHING HE DIDN'T DO TO HELP ME.

SUSAN EVANS

Some nights got so bad that I questioned whether all of this was really worth it since I had been given no guarantees that when this was over the cancer would be gone. George was there to assure me that everything would be fine (why do men always say that when they have no information to prove it?) and that this would all be over soon. (His idea of soon and mine obviously were not the same—soon to me would have been the next hour.)

As I passed the time in bed I noticed how quiet the house was. This home used to be a place of laughter, of discussions over grammar rules (my husband the journalist and me the English teacher often had a difference in opinion over various rules in writing—I always knew that I was right, though) and often with more than one television on at a time. Now there was very little noise-I thought that if I were very still I could just about hear the electricity moving through the wires. It seemed as if the house was sad also.

I got to the point where opening the mail was the highlight of the day—pathetic!

And just when I thought it wouldn't end, it lessened. I could get up and walk around the house, I could start eating food: macaroni and cheese, grilled cheese sandwiches, anything bland, and as my friend said, I was "on the other side" and back in the world. At this point I was amazed that I had lost a few pounds—maybe this was a good plan after all. But the moment I started to feel well enough to eat, I ate, and ate. The dietician had recommended eating a lot of protein, so every three weeks I made the half an hour trip to our favorite beef restaurant (let's just not think about cholesterol at this point).

Just as I felt good, the three weeks were over and it was time to start again.

That's the frustrating part. Just when you start to feel that you can pull yourself off the couch, get dressed and go somewhere, the "somewhere" is back to the chemo lab for another round. But you do it because it has to be done.

Once I got on this three-week chemo schedule, life moved from one three-week block to another. The only real problem? Those stents were still in there! Uncomfortable, irritating, annoying and just plain not good.

Finally the day came when I was "summoned" to an appointment with the urologist. Another trip to Pittsburgh with numerous bathroom stops.

I eagerly walked into that office expecting the stents to be removed.

You just know what happened next—no stent removal!

The doctor drew a picture showing the location of the stents and explaining the procedure that seemed never to be happening and then said I had an infection and the removal would have to be placed on hold.

The tears were back in my eyes and I just couldn't believe that this was happening, or not happening as the case may be.

More green Ditropan pills, more waiting.

As with all things, the waiting did come to an end and I was scheduled for the surgical removal of ONE of the stents. Now why is it that they both went in the same time but they couldn't come out at the same time? Do these medical people enjoy torturing patients?

Another early morning trip to the hospital. By now I had the rules: no food after midnight, no this, no that.

The nurse got me prepped for the procedure, another IV inserted (how long would it be before these veins would just shout "No More!").

The day wore on, and on, and on. No food...we passed noon...no lunch...no water. I got up several times to walk and then back on the bed.

Late afternoon. My patience and that of my husband's had ended hours earlier. We asked several times about the reason for the unending delay and each time we were given some ridiculous, by the-book answer. By now I was ready to get up, get dressed and reschedule.

My urologist appeared, apologized profusely and explained that this was out of his control—something about an anesthesiologist.

Finally, about a minute before I was ready to call hospital administration, or a lawyer (cruel and unusual punishment would hold up in court, I was sure of that) in walked a very tall, white- coated something-or-other. This man (who resembled Ichabod Crane from *The Legend of Sleepy Hollow* and who seemed to be just about as personable as that character) the anesthesiologist in question, pulled back the curtain and said, "How are you today?"

You guessed it, my mouth opened and I replied, "How would you be after lying here for 8 hours with no food or water?"

SUSAN EVANS

Now, any other professional— in this case I use that word loosely— would have tried to ease my feelings. Not this hot shot!

He quickly replied, "I'll leave and then return when you calm down."

And he left.

At that point I could understand why murder could be legal in certain situations.

He did return. Lucky me.

He then began asking me a myriad of questions relating to the reasons that my doctor did whatever he did. Now how was I supposed to know the mind-set of the doctor who had recently saved my life?

STUPIDITY CERTAINLY KNEW NO BOUNDS THAT DAY.

Stupidity certainly knew no bounds that day.

Finally the procedure took place, no problems, no side-effects.

But there still was one more stent to remove.

A week or so later I was to have the other stent removed in the office. I just about danced through the door, anticipating the removal and the ability to not visit the bathroom so frequently.

Of course, nothing was as simple as planned!

As I walked into the exam area there was a young doctor who I had never met. Ever so politely he asked if I would mind if he would remove the stent. At this point I didn't care if the janitor removed the stent, just get it out! However, where was that nice Dr. Jaffee? It seemed that he had burned his hand by reaching for soup in a plastic container in the microwave. Obviously, cooking class was another course not offered in medical school!

The stent was quickly removed, and I now felt better.

And then it was back to the hospital and the tubes and needles. The IV bags hung above my head and I often just watched them drip their poison into my veins. I wondered how many drips a three-hour bag held, but what did it matter? Three, three and a half hours was the rule. It was what it was.

When you spend that many hours sitting you talk with the other women. One woman gave my husband a recipe for soft almond cookies, and one woman told me how her mother had to move to Pittsburgh for a while from Florida to take care of her husband and children. Her reactions to the chemo were quite severe and I was thankful that mine weren't as bad.

There's no way that you could ever imagine that this lab would become a "homey" place, but when you spend that much time in an area it does take on a place of safety, like home. We chatted, exchanged addresses, talked about side-effects and some patients even walked around the area in their socks—just like at home.

The one piece of information that I must have missed or mis-interpreted, was that these treatments are cumulative. The chemicals build up in your system and each treatment has stronger side-effects. So as I lived my life in three-week segments I began to feel worse and not better. More Zofran, more sleep, more aches. I could now move from showers to actual baths but I would be dizzy when trying to get out of the tub. There was my husband with the towels, wrapping me in them and rushing me to the bed. It seemed that the humiliation was also accumulating. Bad enough having internal exams every three weeks, but now I couldn't even get out of the tub on my own. I started to feel that maybe "despair" was a word with which I would become familiar. But as I said before, I wasn't the type to let those demons win this battle. I would win even though I surely was not certain how.

The phone and the computer were my lifelines to the other world, the world I had lived in, enjoying events, going to meetings, lunching with my friends. Since I couldn't do much of my normal activities I could at least talk to people who could.

The treatment schedule crawled along.

Month after month. I made it to a few Steelers' games and I attended a few local meetings. The months wore on and it got closer to my birthday in November. We usually celebrated holidays with our "family" Kathy and Steve, but this year we would by-pass the birthday. Too sick to celebrate.

Christmas, my favorite holiday, was on the horizon and I couldn't fathom how I would be able to decorate (we often had five Christmas trees), bake cookies, shop for gifts, wrap them and plan a dinner. But you know what? It all happened. The trees got up, cookies were baked and gifts were wrapped. The work took way longer than usual but it did get done and there was Christmas in our home.

I found out much later that on the night of my surgery in June that my husband had told Kathy that if the outcome was less than favorable he would have the house decorated and we would have Christmas in September. No need. God works in wondrous ways.

SUSAN EVANS

Finally, the sixth chemo session arrived. I was anxious to get it done and I was joyous to know that this was the end of all of this chemo and that now, finally, I was on my way to a better life.

Wrong again.

Can This Get Any Worse?

I had resigned myself to the cancer and the chemotherapy. The first treatment was a breeze so why should I have thought that they wouldn't all be? My chemo nurse had warned me about the hair loss and had suggested that I go for a wig before my hair started falling out. Never being one to pass up a new shopping experience I visited the nearest, and one of the best, shops in the area that dealt with head coverings. How bad could this possibly be?

Bad.

The woman who greeted me was kind, compassionate, patient and understanding. What do you think I was doing? The usual. Crying!

I sat facing the mirror while she tried various turbans, hats, wigs on my still full head of blond hair. I had to admit that the turbans and hats didn't look too bad. She chatted with me, trying to make me comfortable, told me that she would put me on her prayer chain at her church, gave me advice about keeping a journal, warned me that my hair would start falling out in clumps, and sold me a bag full of head coverings that I was sure I wouldn't need.

I was so sure, that I took the wig part off the day's agenda and went on my way.

After the second chemo treatment I held my breath for days. It looked like the hair was still hanging on, nothing falling out yet.

MY HUSBAND HEARD THE SCREAM

And then one morning, as I came out of the shower, there was a huge clump of hair in my hand.

My husband heard the scream and had visions of the movie *Psycho* where the woman is stabbed in the shower, and he came running. Now, there is nothing good looking about a naked, wet, 64-year-old woman holding a clump of hair and crying. I grabbed a towel. As I looked at him I wondered how much more can this man take? After all, he had a bad heart, actually he had a bad two-thirds of a heart, and my main job in life, as I saw it, was keeping him healthy. Now it seemed the tables were turned, and in my mind it looked like he got the worst end of this deal. Of course, he always disagreed with my assessment. When I had promised, "for better or for worse, in sickness and in health," I had never thought that it would come to this. This man never once questioned his "duty" as a husband; he just felt it was part of life. God did good when he made this one too.

When I could finally breath normally, it's hard to do when you are sobbing (a step up from crying), I realized that it was time to do something about this new torment. Looks like the demons were back again.

On a bright sunny day in July my hairstylist arrived at my home with her tools in hand. I was so appreciative that she came to my home and that I didn't have to have the job done in the salon. I cried, she cut, my husband threw hair in the garbage can. A rather quick process but one that seemed to take forever. No one can relay to you the feelings you have when your head is being shaved. It might have looked good on Demi Moore—but how many of us look like her?

This is another area that I do not think male doctors fully comprehend. Men are used to the idea that eventually they may lose their hair, but women usually are not used to that idea. It is embarrassing to have no hair, on your head or any other area on your body. I looked like a larger version of ET, and not a cute one at that.

The hair was gone and Dana the stylist assured me that I had a perfect head and that I looked beautiful. Now that wasn't something I was believing and when I looked in the mirror I knew that both she and my husband were delusional. The tears came again, along with sounds that I didn't know I could make. I understood "wailing" at that moment. There was nothing beautiful looking back at me from the mirror. But beautiful or not, that's the way it was going to be for quite some time.

The turbans went on and an appointment was made to find a wig.

Now this was a rather costly step. A lot of money for something I didn't want but apparently needed. Something I couldn't imagine wearing but something that might help my self-esteem. No matter how strong you are, and you are strong, when you have no hair you lose self-confidence and you're sure that everyone is looking at you and making comments behind your back. Even though this may not be true, you still feel that way. In your mind it is true. And because you feel it is true the next obstacle arises in your mind: if you just stay in the house no one will notice your new "look."

So you start staying indoors. I sent my husband to the grocery store, there was no way I was going to risk seeing people and explaining to them this entire situation. Church—not going there either for a while. We had a wonderful group of people who we sat with each Sunday but I wasn't venturing there. I could pray at home, God knew where I was, I had been speaking to him non-stop for some time now. Meetings—just mark me absent, I'll get there sooner or later. It was so much easier not to get dressed, stay home and just hide.

Of course this lasted only so long and my husband was referring to me as a "recluse." At one point I was forced to leave the house. The state had decided that my driver's license needed renewed and along with it a new photo had to be taken. Wouldn't you just know that I would have to have this photo with the wig for the next three years to remind me of how bad this was!

Then I gave socializing a try. The first time I went out with my new "friend," the wig, everyone complimented me and said it looked like my real hair. The PAs at the hospital liked it, even my doctor mentioned how nice it looked. I knew they were all trained to say that. What were they going to say, "You look like hell"? At this point I thought the scarves and hats might have been a better idea, but since I bought the wig I might as well use it. No matter where I went I felt uncomfortable. No matter how many people said I looked good, I wrote them off as off-center or just plain nuts. And if they really did think this "look" was good, then how bad had I looked with my real hair?

I wasn't alone with this phobia. While in a chemo session I talked with other younger women who felt the same way. Some of these ladies were young and beautiful but none enjoyed the wig part of this experience. The comments were the same: it itched, it didn't feel natural, it made you self-conscious of your problem, it never felt tight enough, or lose enough, what if it fell off, and on and on. Our only hope was that we had been assured by our respective doctors that our hair would grow back in time.

Of course no one mentioned how much time it would take for our hair to grow back.

There Are Angels Among Us

Through this entire ordeal, and it was an ordeal, I always knew that people were there on the sidelines rooting for me. Just because my husband and I had no family, that didn't mean that we had no people who cared for us. Sometimes you lose sight of the common, everyday things that friends, neighbors, church members, and yes, even mere acquaintances, do for you.

As I dealt with the surgery, the chemo and life on hold, people seemed to be coming out of the woodwork to help me or to give me hope. I found myself wondering how this all could be happening but I knew that that was one of those "why me?" questions that really don't need asked.

One of the very first legions of angels that appeared to help me, and to keep those demons at bay, were, of course, the nurses and the medical staff. Did you ever wonder why nurses and doctors have those white uniforms and coats? I think it's because that's the color the angels wear; I couldn't see the halos but I knew they were there too!

THE NURSES ARE THE UNSUNG **HEROES** OF ANY HOSPITAL...

The nurses are the unsung heroes of any hospital and this particular group was exemplary. From the first night I arrived at Magee until the day I was discharged I received constant attention. I cannot count the times that a nurse would have to come into my room and see why the heart monitor was not working. The leads would come off each time I got out of bed or even moved. Those women were always cheerful and often joked about the lack of adhesive that must be used on these things. Never once did I ask a question, and there were plenty of them, or requested something, that they were not right there with an answer or the item. Time seemed not to be a factor when it came to these women—they always had time for me. I often wondered if I was the only patient on this floor.

They didn't mind that I spent the first few days and nights crying at everything. I guess they were used to that. They constantly reassured me that everything was going as planned. They offered advice to make me more comfortable and they always were pleasant. I doubt that I was always pleasant in my job, so how come they were? Another one of those unanswerable questions.

And let's not forget all of the "helper" aides. They were constantly coming into my room to see how I was doing. They helped me shower and wash my hair. This was not an easy task when I was attached to an IV pole. At times we both looked like we had showered together. They made sure that everything was as good as it could be.

One problem with hospitals, as I see it, is their procurement process. Do they have to go with the very best "deal" when they are purchasing supplies? The toilet tissue left a lot to be desired. There is two-ply, and there is one-ply, and then I think there is institutional ply, which must be about 1/8 ply! After all, this was a woman's hospital, and we women do have standards when it comes to toilet tissue. The staff and I laughed about this and made fun of it, and then in came my aide with REAL toilet tissue. She knew this would make things just a bit better, and she was right. That's the type of people they were, there to help the patient in any way that they could.

SUSAN EVANS

Throughout this entire part of the journey I never felt I was going to die, I never felt bleak. All of these wonderful people at the hospital made sure of that. Everyone always was so positive that it almost seemed like there really wasn't much to worry about. Of course I was afraid of the surgery, the treatments, the side-effects, but never afraid of death. That didn't seem to be an option on the table at the time. It wasn't that I was afraid of dying, we all know that day will come and that day gets closer every minute. It seemed that I wasn't afraid of anything in reality, I was afraid of that all encompassing fear-fear of the unknown. The wonderful staff always helped there. When you have answers to your questions, then the unknown begins to slip away. The more you know and understand the less you are afraid. They made sure of that.

They dealt with the "Go Lightly" product that I had to drink before the colonoscopy. Many suggestions were made about how they could make this more palatable and a few "mixtures" were recommended. Mix it with Crystal Light. That might have worked but since my husband and friend were not available, there was no one to run to a store to purchase some. Mix it with pineapple juice. That could be done. There were all types of juice readily available so that is what we did. This didn't sound too bad until the nurse carried in quite a few pitchers full of ice and juice and told me that I would have to drink every ounce.

Was this type of torture really necessary?

They stopped in all day to make sure that I was drinking and to see if they could make this dire situation any better. Just their concern made it easier.

During my chemo treatments those wonderful women always were there. I am sure that at the end of each day they were exhausted from dealing with so many women and their questions, but never did they show that exhaustion.

The physical therapists, the tech people, even the transportation people, all were as kind as they could be. They always made me feel that I was the most important patient on that floor. Their kindness was genuine. All of this made life in a hospital a bit more tolerable.

One morning as I lay in bed wondering what wretched form of medical abuse could be coming next, in walked the housekeeping person. He was a young man who also tried to make life a bit easier to the patients in the rooms to which he was assigned.

As he pushed his mop over the already pristine floors (this place was immaculate) he asked me where I lived and if I had a job. I told him that I was a retired English teacher and that's when his eyes lit up. He put down the mop, pulled up a chair and took out his Smart Phone. He began to tell me that he wrote poetry and then he read me some of his poems. He also had photos on his phone that illustrated the idea of the poem and he showed me those. We chatted about his poetry, that was quite good, and then he got up to continue his cleaning. Even he had time to talk with me and hopefully I gave him some positive reinforcement about his poetry.

Different doctors appeared in my room each day, all of whom were friendly, non-threatening and positive. I often wondered how many hours do these medical people have in a day and why don't I have the same amount of hours in mine? It must have something to do with time management and dedication.

...PEOPLE WHO I WOULD NOT HAVE THOUGHT EVEN CARED...

After a day or two my room started to resemble a florist shop, or a funeral home, whichever you feel more comfortable picturing. Flowers were arriving from friends, boards that I served on, children of friends, and people who I would not have thought even cared about my health. I appreciated all of these flowers, they made the room more cheerful and gave me something to look at besides the hillsides of Oakland. People who knew I was a Steelers' fan sent the traditional black and gold bouquet. My husband came with red roses.

My mother, who had loved flowers when she was alive, always suggested that we give her flowers while she could enjoy them. Maybe all of these people thought that I was really going to die soon and wanted me to enjoy the arrangements while I still could. Whatever the reason, these senders of flowers were another group of angels who helped me along the route.

And what about friends? If you still have a career, you have a support group who will rally to your side when something like this occurs. Since I had been retired for almost 10 years I felt that I no longer had a support group.

Wrong again.

There were two of my friends, Susan and Greg, peeking around the corner of my door, checking to see if it was all right to enter the room. They had driven an hour after work to visit with me. These were not 20-year friends but were relatively new three-year friends. We had met while serving on the Advisory Board of the University of Pittsburgh at Bradford and had enjoyed many social outings together. They spent time, during that very hot summer night, visiting with me and assuring me that things would go well. They both were very busy people. Greg is an Adult Probation Supervisor and Susan is an Aging Care Management Supervisor. As busy as they were they offered to take vacation days from their very demanding jobs to come to my home and help.

Of course Kathy was always there with her positive outlook on everything—I call my husband and her my Pollyannas, always seeing the bright side of everything.

She sat and sat. She didn't demand that I keep up a conversation, she didn't demand anything other than my keeping a positive attitude. Even after I was discharged and had begun my chemotherapy, she always was there. In the middle of this entire life-changing event she and her entire family went on their annual family vacation. That didn't matter. She was on the phone each day calling to see if I was doing well and offering to come home if I really needed her. She was willing to give up beach and family time to help if necessary. Of course I did not need her to ruin her trip, but the fact that she offered meant more to me than she knew.

This is when you start learning things about yourself. Would I have given up vacation time to help her? I hope that I would.

As time wore on neighbors would arrive at our door with food. Barb, the food consultant in the neighborhood, would send trays of food to our home. My husband was fed and we all were happy. She called daily to see what she could do and she was always there if I needed something.

Some evenings the doorbell would ring and there would be Bill, the CEO of a local organization of which I served on the board, holding a blueberry cobbler that his wife had made. There would be a zucchini bread on the porch. Fran and Judy would come with a peach cobbler, church members Kim and Jenny appeared with a chicken dinner. No way was anyone in this house going to lose weight with friends like these.

One day my husband met a friend as he searched the grocery store for orange popsicles. Remember when you were young and you could buy these frozen treats in a myriad of flavors? Whatever happened to root beer, banana, blueberry and chocolate? Now there's yogurt bars, Italian ices, fruit bars, but no selection of flavors for popsicles!

While enduring the after-effects of the chemo treatments I always craved something cold and popsicles did the job. However, George was forced to purchase the variety box just to get a few orange ones. Our friend, Patty, offered to buy a couple of boxes right there, open them up and trade the flavors so that I would have a complete box of orange ones.

So many offers of kindness will come your way. Accept them—don't say "no" to those who are trying to help you. You will need help. Meals will not get prepared when you can't even get out of bed. Laundry will not do itself if your husband has no idea of how to turn on the washer. Sooner or later you will need clean towels and sheets and you will not be able to do it. Allow others to help you.

Lap blankets and prayer blankets started arriving. Up until this point I am not sure that I even knew what one of those were. Apparently, women who have chemo treatments feel cold. Now I understood why my chemo nurse was always asking me if I needed a blanket and I was always assuring her that I did not. You will be surprised at the number of organizations that provide these hand-made blankets to chemo patients. I know that I was. My church, St. Bernard's, has a group of women who make the prayer blankets, complete with a small book of prayers tucked in the pocket. Up until my illness I did not even know that the church did this.

If you have children and perhaps grandchildren, let them take over. That's a fearful phrase, "take over," but that's what will need to be done. I, the Type A personality, did not like that idea at all, but my husband had to be given full reign of the house. In my mind, I now was going to die from a nervous breakdown because I knew that nothing would be done to my specifications. I would have to get a grip on the situation and accept this new division of labor. There's that prayer of St. Francis cropping up again.

Getting to those Steelers' games was a priority and the first Sunday, that opening day that I had been so worried about when I had first been admitted to the hospital, arrived—and so had I at Gate B. As I was checked by security, the woman noticed, even though I had a scarf covering my head, that I obviously had no hair. She concluded that I had cancer and she asked if I needed help getting to my seat. She offered the elevator, I declined, and reached my level on my own. As I started to ascend those steps that Mike the scan-man had said I would conquer, the usher asked me if I knew where my seat was located. I politely told him that I had been sitting in these seats for over 10 years. He, too, noticed that I had a health problem and he said, "And we hope that you are with us for at least 10 more years." The concern from the staff was heartwarming.

And never underestimate the concern of people who hardly know you even though you spend four hours on eight fall and winter Sundays with them.

As season ticket holders for the Steelers' games we have our "friends" in our seat section. A young man, who we all call "Dancing Robbie" because he dances and keeps the audience entertained throughout the games, noticed (how could he not) that I had a new "look." No hair, a scarf and hat, suntan lotion and not the usual boisterousness that my football friends have come to know about me.

SUSAN EVANS

He and our longtime friend and seat-mate went for a beer and he asked our friend, also named Rob, what had happened. After he heard the story he said he felt very bad for me. Rob, our friend, said, "Don't count her out. She's one of the strongest people you will ever meet."

As they returned to their seats the young man climbed over a row or two to get to me, gave me a kiss and said he would be praying for me. At each subsequent game he would give me the heart thump and look to the sky. He always wanted to know how I was doing. He would ask me several times, just in case I was lying to him. Almost a total stranger and now in my heart for life.

As you live through this, and you will live through it, you will find that even your local pharmacist will check in with you to see how you are doing. It's absolutely amazing how many people you never knew will ask about your health.

I had been placed on just about every prayer chain in this town as well as in Pittsburgh. Anyone who knew anyone would place my name on that church's prayer chain. I guess I was covered for any and all circumstances. Just knowing that people are praying for you helps. I truly believe that prayer never hurts anything; we always can use some help from someone or something higher than us.

On a Sunday that I was able to get to church the Eucharistic minister held my hand while she gave me communion. That brought tears to my eyes. Again, you may wonder how many times you have prayed for people on your church's prayer chain. The kindness of strangers was all around me. Hopefully, in the years to come, I also could extend that kindness to others.

THE KINDNESS OF STRANGERS WAS ALL AROUND ME.

When I had gone to buy my scarves and wig, the kind woman who helped me suggested that I start a journal at that point and that I write down everything that happens and who sends cards or brings food or does any act of charitable kindness toward me and my husband. I did not follow her advice but I did keep all of the cards and notes that were sent to me. I also made sure that I sent thank-you notes to everyone. I am a firm believer in formally thanking people. Write those notes, if nothing else it will give you something to do when you are recovering. When you look back on this experience you will be amazed at all who tried, and did, help you.

Once I was home more flowers started to arrive. What cheer they brought to me. It was summer and I did not feel well enough to even go out on the patio, so the flowers in the house at least offered some summer indoors.

SUSAN EVANS

Friends came to visit when I felt a bit better. They offered encouragement and helped to just pass the time. Once you are home from the hospital the days pass much more slowly. There's not the constant attention of the medical staff nor the constant interruptions of your sleep. Accept those visits from your friends and remember that someday you will be the visitor to someone else who needs encouragement.

It will be the small things that you will remember. They are the events that happened that really did not amount to a great deal but that helped at a particular moment to make you feel better about yourself. Treasure them.

As the Christmas season approached so did the holiday parties. Although I still had to wear the wig I did feel well enough to attend a few events. On one occasion, our friends Steve and Kathy accompanied us to a party. Steve, who is a man of few words, looked at me and told me that I looked really good. He joked that perhaps I had not had a problem and that maybe Kathy and I had been shopping in Pittsburgh all of those days the previous summer. His words made me feel so good. I did not feel that I looked good, this "thing" was still resting on my head, but just the fact that he thought to say it helped. Another angel.

And then there was the day I met my doctor in the hospital lobby. There he was, again looking like he had no sleep in recent history, standing in line in his light blue scrubs, a Pitt hoodie, totting a huge shoulder bag, at the ATM machine. We exchanged pleasantries and then he said, "You look wonderful. You certainly don't look like a patient who needs me."

Now, of course, maybe he says that to everyone. Who knows what they are taught in medical school? But that didn't matter.

I am sure that he had no idea how that bolstered my self-confidence. Those few words made my day. But I already knew that he was an angel.

The prayer of St. Francis de Sales is one which I was not familiar with but am now. *"Make yourself familiar with the angels, and behold them frequently in spirit; for without being seen, they are present with you."* Through all of this you will have those angels who are both seen and unseen.

No matter where you look, those angels will be there to assist you on this journey. Realize their presence and rely on them whenever you need to. You are not going through this alone, no matter how it feels some days.

Remember the line from the play *A Streetcar Named Desire*. Blanche DuBois says, "I have always been dependent on the kindness of strangers."

For a while, so will you.

SUSAN EVANS

15 More

Again, I kept asking myself, "how wrong can I be?" Obviously there was no limit to my naivete when it came to these medical situations.

This was to be the last exam for a while and the last chemo treatment.

Chemo done, or so I thought. As I sat in the exam room I imagined my life getting back to normal. It started to look like this trip would soon be completed.

Just like on a highway, the detour sign appears unexpectedly.

In walked not only the PA but the doctor and the chemo nurse right with her. Obviously either something was wrong or there was some type of information going to be disseminated that just one person didn't feel comfortable doing. Funny how the time schedules allowed three professionals this day.

The exam went well, the marker number was fine, no problems anywhere.

The doctor sat on the counter and began to tell me that he would like me to undergo 15 treatments of this chemical called Avastin (Bevacizumab); one treatment every three weeks. I looked at my husband with those tears in my eyes again. He affirmed that "we"—there's that "'we'" again—would do anything we had to do to make sure that I was healthy. Again, why do men think that everything is fine? Let them try this chemo business for a while and we'll see if they would sign up for 15 more treatments. In my mind I was thinking, no more of this, I'm done, I can't do anymore.

Mr. Nice Doctor said that he thought he had mentioned this to me before and that he guessed he had "sand bagged" (his term not mine) me on this. No kidding! Maybe I had judged him incorrectly and just maybe he was working for some demonic torture organization! After a few seconds of just trying to breath, he explained to me that some new clinical trial data had been completed and that the use of additional Avastin therapy was beneficial. He stated, "This is how I would treat my family members." Now who is going to argue with that?

But these treatments were a question of choice. I did not have to do them, there would be little if any side-effects and once they were started they would only take 30 minutes. He explained that some women choose not to do them and that the decision was up to me. (Hadn't I just heard my husband say we would do them? Where was the choice???) The chemo nurse encouraged me to do them, so did the PA. The overall survival rate for me would be better so why not give it a try? I also was told that if I didn't like doing the treatments I could stop at any time.

It was explained that this type of therapy would not make me sick as the other chemo did. The doctor explained the treatments by saying that if you wanted to kill someone, you could lock him in a closet and starve him to death or you could just shoot him. Either way, the person would be dead. The Avastin would work the same way and "starve" a tumor if one was to develop. It targets the blood vessels, it is called targeted chemo, and that is one reason that I would not have the severe side effects that I had with the first set of chemo treatments.

Now this explanation I could understand. Why couldn't all medical procedures be explained in plain English like this one?

But 15 treatments, one every three weeks, sounded interminable. That was 45 more weeks of this running back and forth and having infusions. It looked like more trips would have to be cancelled but I was assured that the treatments could be scheduled around my life and not the other way around.

Great. Sign me up—one more new experience coming up!!

Every three weeks I had labs done and made the trip to the hospital. The experience, once again, was made as pleasant as possible by all of the personnel who helped me. TV, lunch, and you're ready to go home. I never got to view an entire television program; a half hour moves very quickly.

NOTHING COMPARED TO THE SIDE EFFECTS OF THE PREVIOUS SIX CHEMO TREATMENTS.

As I sat in the chair and watched the IV bag drip-again, how many "drips" were in that small bag? I considered myself very lucky. There were women who obviously were suffering a lot more than I was, and even a few men, but no one seemed to complain. Once in awhile things did not go as planned. One day the needle hit something in my vein and it had to be removed and started again. This hurt, a lot, but the nurse tried her best to get it right. I figured by this time my veins were rebelling-they had had enough.

My doctor hadn't lied. There were no side-effects. It was possible that as the treatments progressed I could see a rise in my blood pressure and I could have nosebleeds. Nothing compared to the side-effects of the previous six chemo treatments.

And then another problem. I needed a root-canal! For anyone who has had one of these you know that they are not pleasant to say the least. The road-block now was that I couldn't have the root-canal while on the Avastin. Everything came to a screeching halt.

As if this were not bad enough, this type of procedure needed to be done not in our town but in Erie, Pa. So off to Erie it was. Then a permanent filling had to be done and of course my dentist chose that week to go on vacation. I was handed off to a strange dentist. With a lot of work and pain the job was done. One more hurdle jumped and then back to the regular schedule.

Don't think that everything will go as planned—it doesn't, no matter how hard you try or how hard you try to control things. Remember, you have no control.

I noticed that there was a "lump" that had formed along my incision line. Now that was cause for concern. Should I tell my PA or just ignore it and hope that if this was another problem perhaps I could just pretend it wasn't there!

At my next exam I waited until she was done and then I mentioned it. She, and Chris, said it was normal and often happened after surgery-a hernia-great!!! Karen said that she has had one for 15 years and not to worry about it now. A lump, and I am supposed to not worry?? This medical business seems to have few black and white answers, just a lot of gray.

Everything then fell into the original time-frame.. My life was back to a normal routine, I felt great, and I lived on the three-week schedule. Now I was sure that everything would go along normally until I had completed the 15 treatments.

You guessed it, wrong again!

About half way through the Avastin course my doctor informed me that he was changing hospitals. That was fine, I thought. He assured me that he still would be my doctor. That made me feel even better. Everyone is entitled to change jobs, good for him. However, that did not cover the entire situation.

Apparently, doctors have the "do not compete" clause in their contracts which made him unable to work in Allegheny County. So, although he still would be my doctor I would have to find another facility to have my treatments. That meant leaving those wonderful people at the hospital who had been taking such good care of me for almost the past year. More trauma!

I was to be sent to another facility—okay I guess. I was not too pleased with this and of course I expressed that to Dr. Tom. Not that he didn't have enough on his mind. Now he had this patient who didn't want to switch facilities. That too was a choice. I could stay at Magee and have my treatments there, and be assigned a new doctor, or I could go with him. Now really, what type of choice was that? You don't change horses in the middle of a stream nor was I going to change doctors in the middle of treatments.

Another bump in the road.

I was assigned a new doctor at the new facility. I made sure that he would be considered the secondary doctor, not the primary. I might be agreeing to this change but not without my usual attitude.

The decision to follow the doctor was a very hard one to make. If and when you may be put in this position remember to put yourself first. We all become attached to our caregivers, but do not make any decisions because of this attachment. Think of what might be best for you and your family. Think about any inconvenience a change may cause. Think about your having to develop a new mind-set with another group of medical professionals. Remember that the building is not as important as the person treating you. You do not stay somewhere because of bricks and mortar, you stay to get the best care available at the time.

The time came to leave all of the wonderful people at Magee who had been taking care of me. This was more than difficult, this was heart wrenching. My husband was waiting for a day full of tears, and he just about got it.

We had decided to bring the office lunch that day and I had all to do to keep from crying when I carried in the trays. These people had been so good to me for almost a year and now I felt like I was abandoning them!

My PA came in the exam room, did the exam and then sat down to talk. She talked, I cried. She reassured me that the new place was going to be fine and that if I was not happy I was to return to her. She also said that she would always be there, just call if I had any questions. Apparently, they do not abandon the patient when the patient jumps ship!

And then my chemo nurse, wonderful Chris, joined the love fest. We talked, hugged, cried together and she, too, assured me that they were not setting me adrift with no lifeline. She would always be there for me and she would call me periodically to see how I was doing.

Now all of this was meant to make me feel better, but I still felt guilty that I was leaving them.

Then it was on to the chemo section to get my treatment. More tears, more goodbyes.

And then I walked out of that wonderful hospital to face a new set of people who supposedly would take care of me as well as Magee had.

Three weeks passed and it was time to get the next treatment-this time at the new facility. I had been assured that this new place was "swanky" as my one PA put it, and the kind doctor was sure that I was going to get even nicer treatment than I had been used to—okay, I figured I could give it a try.

The night before the treatment the demons found me again and got to work on my mind. My long suffering husband had to tolerate another night of ranting. I began the tirade at about 1a.m.

"I don't want to go to this new place. I'm going to hate it, the people won't be as nice as those wonderful people at Magee."

He tried to sleep.

I kept the tirade going. (If I were a politician I would have been excellent at the filibuster.)

"Why do I have to do this? Everything was perfect the way it was. I'm going to hate it."

He sleepily replied, "You had a choice, keep the doctor and change the facility or change the doctor and keep the facility."

"I don't care!" I just about shrieked.

"Then don't do it and let me sleep! Call your doctor right now and tell him how you feel, I'm up, he might as well be too." (Now where's the empathy he had shown for the past year?) Obviously the choice was made and the next morning we were off to find the new place.

As I stamped (spoiled child syndrome) down the hall to the office my husband followed behind humming *"Hail To The Chief"*—and you thought the tune was only for presidents! I pointed out that this was not helping the situation.

At times like this when George knows that a tornado is about to land in someone's life he often stands back a few paces (something about the line of fire) and just watches the situation unfold. We often play the good-cop/bad-cop routine.

I entered the reception area and was assaulted by noise and movement. The place was packed, the TV was blaring and there were people everywhere. Obviously I had chosen one of the busier days to begin this new experience.

I gave the harried receptionist my name, she told me to wait, (people really need to say "Hello, how are you today?" before anything else) not my strong suit, and finally handed me an "information" folder and told me it would be a while.

Now you know what happened next.

My mouth opened, again, and I informed her that I didn't plan on waiting long. I had never waited at the other facility and I didn't plan on starting now. I also threw in the "my time is as valuable as yours".

SUSAN EVANS

Quite quickly a technician called me into the exam room. She was a cute, young woman who probably considered a career change by the time I was finished.

She took my blood pressure, which was unusually very high (no kidding) and then told me I would have a long wait because the doctor who was assigned to me was in a conference.

You guessed it again.

I told her to find the woman I had spoken to on the phone several times and who had led me to believe that this transition would run smoothly. I assumed that this woman was an office manager or an administrative assistant of some type.

When she entered the room I noticed that she had a stethoscope around her neck and I was pretty sure that a clerical person was not issued this equipment. Was she an office manager? Nope. She was a medical professional, in gold flip-flops and denim capri pants. I realized that everyone in this office complex wore jeans, t-shirts, sneakers or sandals. It then dawned on me that this probably was a dress-down Friday. Now during my 32-year career I was never a fan of the dress-down idea-high school was usually casual enough. Certain places have no dress-down days—have you ever seen a law enforcement official (police) dressed "down" on a certain day? Do you think the FBI or CIA offices have dress-down days? That type of casual attitude is not to my liking, but there it was. The clothing does not influence the type of treatment that you get at a medical facility, but

CHANGE IS HARD.

it does affect the attitude and the feeling of confidence that some patients have. I got past the dress code and this nice woman listened to me as I gave her the litany of reasons why I didn't want to be here. Change is hard. She explained their protocol and jokingly told me that I was going to like it there.

After our discussion and a few laughs (they are good at calming your nerves and that was what this was all about) it was off to the treatment room.

I was disappointed. At Magee I was treated like a queen, as were all of the women patients. Here there were no separate cubicles, everyone in large groups, no massage chairs, no one bringing snacks/beverages. The snacks were available but no one ever bothered to tell me that until I was ready to leave. Communication is very important when a person is a "first timer" at a facility. People were talking over the half-walls; noise, movement, too much sensual stimulation for me. There were large windows—couldn't I just jump???

Everyone is different and I am sure others liked the open concept and the chatting with others—too much noise for me.

SUSAN EVANS

Change can be either positive or negative. It is only negative when you are UNABLE (I was not, I could accept this) UNWILLING (now there's where I was) or UNPREPARED (I knew what to expect, to an extent, so I guess this part was out too). It looked like I would have to suck it up and continue at this location.

The bottom line: the nurses were kind and gentle, I had my treatments and I left each time knowing that this would not be forever.

I don't need to repeat the conversation, but what do you think the nice, young doctor heard when I spoke with him later that day??!!

The next treatment was worse than the first. Frustration set in and the tears came. I was used to hugs and smiles and good manners—it just wasn't the same.

As the weeks wore on the next obstacle seemed to be getting my marker number. It seems that although you have the blood work done no-one is too quick to give you the results, even to the point of asking, "Why do you even want to know this number?"

Now let's make a giant point here and let's hope that the medical profession listens. It's my blood work, it's my number and I'm paying for it. There is not even a plausible reason why ANYONE should even ask why I want it. It's mine!!! So speak up and don't just sit there and give someone an explanation- they don't deserve one.

Things eventually ironed themselves out—still no hugs or "Hello, how are you today?" How was your trip?" But I knew that this was only going to last for a short time and then I would be finished with the treatments and this facility.

If you are faced with a change through treatments try to be more tolerant than I was. I set the bar high for myself and thus for everyone else also. That sets me up for disappointment a lot. The strength that I showed during this change and the difficult decisions that the system had me make again posed an obstacle that showed me that I could overcome anything as I fight this on-going battle with cancer. The bottom line was that these were my choices, no matter how limited those choices were, and I was in charge—not the cancer and not my doctor. We all worked as a team. Some studies show that the people who are on your team-family, friends, medical professionals, everyone who helps you get through this crisis are almost as important as the medicine itself. The problem was that I didn't want to be part of this new "team" and I did not feel that my "teammates" were as concerned about me as my former ones were.

However, as any professional athlete knows, sometimes you're on the team but you don't want to be. You dress for the game but you're waiting to be traded. That's how I felt. I'll play the game but get me out off this new "team" as soon as possible.

During these Avastin treatments my doctor started mentioning the possibility that he might keep me on them for another year or so. This in itself was fine with me. If a new study proved that more treatments were beneficial then I could do them—but we would have to find another facility. I was not about to be frustrated with this facility for another 15 treatments. He assured me that he would find another place. I knew he didn't want to hear my complaints and deal with my tears for another year. I also stated (no more asking–I really was taking this into my own hands) that before I committed to another facility I wanted a tour of the chemo area. He assured me that this could be arranged when and if the time came.

Post-Traumatic Stress Disorder

The Mayo Clinic defines post-traumatic stress disorder (PTSD) as a mental health condition that is triggered by a terrifying event. Symptoms may include flashbacks, nightmares and/or severe anxiety, as well as uncontrollable thoughts about the event.

Many people who go through traumatic events (wars, fires, floods, earthquakes, etc.) have difficulty adjusting and coping for a while. This becomes a problem when the symptoms do not get better over time or the symptoms get worse. Although you are not dealing with the common causes of this disorder, you are dealing with a life-threatening medical diagnosis, cancer, which can be just as traumatic to you as a natural disaster, plane crash, assault or civil conflict. Do not try to minimize the problem—try to deal with it.

These types of symptoms are generally grouped into three types: intrusive memories, avoidance and numbing, and increased anxiety or emotional arousal (hyperarousal).

You may never have thought of this disorder until you were diagnosed with cancer, but when you look back on your diagnosis and surgery you may agree that you have gone through a traumatic event. Being told that I had a 25-pound tumor was rather traumatic. Thinking I had a swollen ankle only to discover that I had ovarian cancer also was quite traumatic. Anxiety certainly would be understandable in these cases.

... NOT TALKING ABOUT IT... DOESN'T MAKE IT GO AWAY.

Some women find that they can avoid the entire subject just by not talking about it—that doesn't make it go away. You may get to the point where you become emotionally numb, and rightly so. From the time I was diagnosed until the surgery, only a few days, I was in a whirlwind. Tests, kidney stents, filters for blood clots, take this, drink that, go for a scan, lab work, one thing after another with little if any time to think. You do become emotionally numb. I think the medical profession likes the patient that way because it cuts down on questions and comments, but not on tears and fears.

You may avoid activities that you like. No kidding. For a while you can't even get out of bed without feeling nauseous. You have no hair, wigs itch, and you don't have the strength to do much.

Some of the frequently asked questions about your feelings may be:

Do you avoid certain people, places or situations that remind you of the traumatic experience?

You may avoid your check-ups at your doctor's office because it brings back thoughts of your diagnosis. You may avoid ever entering a hospital because it makes you relive a traumatic medical experience. Often women avoid their yearly gynecological exams because of poor treatment in the past. Going to the gynecologist is not the most pleasant experience in your life—the dentist might rank higher, but if you find the right doctor it just might not be as bad.

Do you often feel irritable or angry?

It is normal to have these feelings in life but if they are caused by your recent surgery, and if they linger for a long time, you will have to deal with them. You may want to list the things that anger you. Make the list and then deal with each —can you do anything to fix or eliminate the cause of the anger? If you are angry that you have cancer, that you have had surgery, that you don't think it's fair that it has happened to you, then mentally examine what you can do about these things. In my mind, that answer would be "not much." You have cancer, you are being treated hopefully by the best doctor you could find and as far as "fair" is considered, forget it. Life isn't fair, work around that point and try to look at all of the good things which you have in your life.

Again, don't let your attitude control you and don't try to change the things that can't be changed. Some people feel that they are constantly "on-guard" for any sign that they have recurring cancer. Don't let every ache or pain move you to run to the phone or to call your doctor. If something really feels wrong, by all means, let the doctor know. That's why the doctor's there. Don't sit at the computer and research every form of cancer and its symptoms. Remember you are unique, you are not the general population, you are you.

Have you been having trouble in your personal relationships?

PTSD can affect not just you but all of those around you. It's not a one-person disorder. No matter how hard your friends, relatives, family members try, they will never know what it was like to hear "You have cancer" in the same way that you did. We all react differently, and although your friend may have had a cancer diagnosis, her feelings were not the same as yours. Your family can try to empathize but they will never feel exactly as you do.

Don't try to force anyone to think exactly as you do. You have your feelings and others have their's; work within those parameters. Don't push people away, keep them close enough to help you when you need them.

Trouble concentrating and memory problems also are indicators of PTSD.

These should pass and before long you should be back to normal. For the longest time I couldn't concentrate on reading or on my stitching, the two activities I really enjoy. Eventually I regained interest, and the ability to concentrate. Once I started to physically feel better I emotionally felt better too.

At some point you may feel hopeless about the future, another sign.

It often is difficult to find the silver lining when you feel nauseous, ache all over and have no energy. You see the days slipping away and you do not seem to be part of those days. It is easy to fall into the "poor me" trap—but don't! All of this passes and hopefully in time you will feel fine.

Don't let those demons take over–you're stronger than they are.

It's important to follow your health professional's instructions. Take care of yourself. Get enough rest, eat a balanced diet, take time to relax, avoid caffeine and nicotine which can worsen anxiety. Don't self-medicate.

A support group of people who have gone through what you have might help. Meditation, yoga, or just long walks could help you see things more calmly and help you to progress.

As I was progressing through the stages of my cancer treatment I tried to remain positive. I am the type of person who has no time for self-pity and I viewed this as a "bump" in the road. I followed all of the directions which were given to me. I kept my appointments and treatments on a regular three-week schedule and in between I had a life to live. I spent no time wallowing in self-pity—you get nowhere doing that. I moved on.

It is easy to offer advice, especially if you have never experienced something. Everyone who doesn't have children is an expert in child behavior. But I have experienced the shock, the trauma, the fear of cancer so I can offer some advice. You need to fight. Cancer will only win if you let it win. A positive attitude is your first step to recovery—after that things will take care of themselves.

I vaguely remember a part of a song lyric that sums up this whole "think positive" approach—"Spread your arms, take a breath and always trust your cape." You can fly.

Coping with the Sword of Damocles

If you have never heard of the "Sword of Damocles" it is a story written by Cicero in ancient Rome. Those ancient Romans had a handle on this stuff. A short summary would be that the entire story can be summed up in "Judge no man until his life is over,"a familiar theme in Greek and Roman philosophical writing. To use an English idiom, we would say, "walk a mile in my shoes."

To paraphrase the story, Dionysius (II) was a fourth century B.C. tyrant of Syracuse, the Greek area of southern Italy. To all appearances he had everything. He even had court flatterers to inflate his ego. One of these was Damocles. Damocles often would make comments about what a great life Dionysius had. One day when Damocles complimented the tyrant on his abundance and power, Dionysius said, "If you think I'm so lucky, how would you like to try out my life?"

Damocles agreed and Dionysius ordered everything to be prepared for Damocles to experience this new life. Damocles was greatly enjoying himself, until he noticed a sharp sword hanging over his head, that was suspended from the ceiling by a horsehair. This, the tyrant explained, was what life was really like.

Damocles suddenly revised his idea of what made a good life, and asked to be excused. He then returned to his poorer, but safer life.

Everyone seems to think that someone who is richer or prettier or more famous than they lives a better life. If we could trade for a day we would find that those people may have more problems than we do. Therefore, again, do not feel sorry for yourself. There will be people worse off than you sitting in that chemo lab that would love to trade their lives at that moment for yours. Cancer of any kind knows no economic, religious, ethnic or any other boundaries.

The sword always will be there hanging over your head. The fear of a recurrence always will be there. There are days when the reality of having cancer never entered my mind. I felt wonderful. And then the thought-those demons again-is back in my head. You will never have that 100% feeling that you are in good health again, even though you may be. There's that sword again.

WE ARE NOT JUST A CANCER PATIENT.

We are all someone's wife, mother, sister, daughter, friend; we are not just a cancer patient.

It's not easy, but it's your life, be happy that you have been granted more time and cope with what you have. There's St. Francis again: *"accept the things you cannot change."*

Throughout this whole journey, day by day, I had to cope. Not one day was perfect, most were not easy, but I still had to get through them. Each day required focusing on the positive and on good things that were happening. Choose the right foods during treatments, plan to live a healthier lifestyle, this is when you have the time to plan.

There are thousands of ways to cope with problems, we all know that. Now it was time to find the ones that really would help me.

SUSAN EVANS

While undergoing the first six chemo treatments I read where taking a walk or going outside for a while would help with the unpleasant symptoms. I would suggest that whoever writes these suggestions needs to be someone who has gone through these treatments and not someone who has researched what "seems" to work.

Go outside? Take a walk? I couldn't get from the bed to the bathroom without help on most days, and someone wants me to get dressed and go for a walk?

Fresh air? It was an extremely hot summer and the only air I wanted was the air coming from the air-conditioner.

Obviously these suggestions weren't working for me, but they may for you.

Hours, days, weeks, with very little to do but lie in bed. That's when you start to just think and that's when you have to find a way to believe that you will get better and this too will pass. I found that it helped to maintain an attitude of gratitude. Do not spend your time being pessimistic, it doesn't get you anywhere. When I was especially uncomfortable or annoyed or in pain I would keep in mind that there would be tomorrow, or at least I hoped there would be, and that today I was here, being taken care of by numerous people and indeed blessed at that moment. Taking one day at a time is a good option, but if you have to take just one minute at a time, you will find that that works too.

While you're just thinking about things, think about the passage from the book The Hotel New Hampshire where the character Fanny appears sad and someone asks her if they can do anything for her. She says, "Just bring me yesterday, and most of today."

You're going to feel that way. Yesterday-before cancer-was great! And maybe part of this particular day was also. Fine. Reminisce and then move on. It will never be like "yesterday" again, so don't wish it. Look to the future when you will be able to do what you like to do.

When the worst of the chemo was over I had to readjust. For a while. I was not strong enough to jump back into my normal routine and I could not do all of the things in my home that I was used to doing. You will find that you still need to rest, but now, maybe, you can go for a short walk, or just sit on your porch and enjoy the sun and the fresh air. How many times did I take these small pleasures for granted? I won't anymore, I am sure.

Take time to do the things you love—play with your children, or grandchildren. We were blessed with Kathy's daughter,

Rachel, having her baby and just holding that little one gave me happiness.

Walk the dog, talk with your neighbors. In my case all of the neighbors had been concerned about me throughout the ordeal and they all were happy to see me at the mailbox or in my yard.

Remember all of those saints that I had called upon for help? Maybe now was a good time to spend some time thanking them for the good results. Meditation isn't a bad way to stay calm and focused either.

Bake, cook, sew, do whatever you like. I would bake for the stylists at my hair salon, they're on their feet all day and they appreciated the "treats"—helping others has its own rewards.

Get out of your nightgown or pajamas. You will feel a lot better if you look a lot better. Get dressed, put on your make-up, do your nails, get a pedicure, get your hair cut.

During one of my exams my PA noticed my handbag, one day my shoes, one day my jewelry. She always complimented me and once said that if she were coming for chemo she probably would roll out of bed and jump into her sweat pants. I always felt that if I looked the best that I could I would feel much better. There's no use looking like you were dragged

through hell, even though you had been. You might be suffering emotionally at this time but you don't have to make
everyone else suffer.

Some people like photos, some do not. I am one of the "do
nots". One way of moving on is to trick yourself into thinking that the entire situation wasn't as bad as it really was. I
have only one photo of me, with the wig, and that was only
because I was holding Rachel's baby and we wanted a picture
of her, not me. With no photos there are no reminders-ok
with me! As mentioned before, however, I do have a new
driver's license from that time period, and although those
photos are never the most attractive, this one of me with the
wig really was bad. Everyone always jokes that those state
taken photos could be used if a person were sent to prison
or just arrested-they're that bad. Now, don't get me wrong,
there was nothing wrong with the wig, it was nice, everyone
seemed to like it (what were they going to say??) But, it just
wasn't me.

I doubt that the Commonwealth of Pennsylvania would
understand, so I guess I keep the photo license.

Go out to eat. If you can, go somewhere really nice and
somewhere that is your favorite place. Don't hide from
people-I had done that when I lost my hair and it hadn't made
me feel any better.

SUSAN EVANS

So what if you can't finish your meal; take it home and eat it the next day.

As the months wear on you will find yourself falling back into your old routine. By this time, if you have a career, you will have been back to work and probably enjoying it a lot more than you used to.

There may be a topic that needs to be addressed at this point, one which may or may not be relevant to you depending on your age (although I do not feel age has much to do with it).

Here comes that other word that we usually don't feel comfortable discussing with strangers—

SEX.

I have been told by several doctors that sometimes the husbands, boyfriends, significant others, are afraid to have intimate relations because they are concerned that they may injure their partner.

So ladies, if you're interested in this extracurricular activity you better tell your partner that it's okay. Most men, or women, aren't going to catch on too quickly to this, so if you don't guide them toward your desired result you may be waiting until forever.

Some women have discussed this with their medical professional (I'm not making this up, I asked several doctors) and were concerned about pain during intercourse, lubrication problems, you get the idea. One doctor said that men like to brag about penis size (this is where my deceased mother is saying, "You are NOT saying the word 'penis' in this book!") and that's often what women think causes the pain. He said that the real reason is that

...IF YOU DON'T GUIDE THEM... YOU MAY BE WAITING UNTIL FOREVER.

the lining of the vagina thins and that is what may contribute to the uncomfortable feeling during intercourse. Once again, why is it always about the men?! Talk about it to people who can help you-medical people, not your phone friends or the ladies at the beauty salon.

On the opposing side, I have spoken with women who have revealed that they cannot get enough of "it". One woman thought that perhaps her partner would be dead before these constant urges passed.

Everyone is different. I guess you have to figure this part out on your own. Some sexual partners might need a little guidance.

SUSAN EVANS

A Husband's Perspective

Allow me to begin by saying that I am a journalist. Supposedly I am a man of words, yet I have never written a novel, a fiction piece, a poem, or a love letter. Now I am writing about something that happened to the only someone who has meant everything to me. To express my feelings, I feel like the proverbial shoemaker without a pair of shoes.

For all of you husbands, boyfriends, brothers, significant others, none of this will be easy. It wasn't for me. Hearing the word "cancer" and realizing that it involved my wife made my heart sink to my stomach. However, I could not show her how I felt-I had to be her support-someone for her to lean on during this unexpected journey.

YOU DON'T ASK, YOU JUST DO.

None of what I say about Susan's ordeal comes easy, other than my love for her that strengthens more and more each day of our 40 years together. With such a lasting partnership, I learned that you don't ask, you just do.

I didn't question her pain. I cried.

I never questioned my love, yet I questioned over the years my attention to it. My fault.

I didn't question the doctor's treatment. I trusted.

I raised the "why her" question, but she never raised the "why me" one. I know it's unanswerable.

My heart took a heart-attack beating 10 years ago, but it has taken a pounding with Sue's bout with cancer.

Detecting my feelings is detective work, yet this time a five year old could uncover them. From the moment Sue's swollen ankle catapulted into ovarian cancer, my heart pounded non-stop like a bass drum. All I could think of was a local (rural) doctor referring to the 25-pound tumor and forecasting doom and death within six months. I could feel my heart rate rising by the second. How long would it take for the defibrilator to go off?

After more than a year after the initial surgery, I can say that I no longer worry about my heart. I am grateful for the superb medical care that Sue has received in Pittsburgh–her home. Yet I always will be vigilant even at the sound of her sneeze and drive her crazy by asking her over and over if she's all right.

Throughout Susan's story, there are two sentences that capture her determination. "You need to fight. Cancer will only win if you let it win."

Throughout Sue's 13 days at Magee, I grew more and more impressed with her mental and physical strength. She never complained. She remained upbeat, and because of that so did I. I became more and more impressed with the attentive staff—no facades among any of them. They were the real deal. I initially was impressed with Dr. Krivak because his treatment suggestions always were phrased with "among our recommendations." That word "our" led me to believe that her care was a teamwork endeavor.

What impressed me more than anything else ever could was Susan's endurance under very intolerable circumstances. Those Lovonox injections twice daily for six months created a sea of deep purple bruises over her stomach and her thighs.

SUSAN EVANS

If a seventh month was necessary, I would not have been sure where I could inject the needles. She never complained. If it were me, I would have yelled for mercy.

The side-effects of her chemotherapy erupted into countless restless nights the week after each of the six treatments. I could not stand her in any pain, but she stood the test. I was the weakling.

Among my many failings—I have many, believe me—is that I too often, and wrongly, see the darker side than the brighter one. This is where Sue and I differ, dramatically. As dim as the light may have been at the time, she always saw the bright spot. Never did she think there would not be a tomorrow due to cancer. She believed. I did not believe at first, even with Dr. Krivak's assurance after the surgery that her cancer was "treatable" and "probably curable." After all this time though, and the progress that Sue has made, I truly do believe in a brighter light.

I know that Sue was running on adrenalin and instinct, then and now. So am I. I doubt that you ever can say it's over.

My head was in a whirlwind that first night when she was taken by ambulance to Magee. I am not sure how I got there as quickly as the ambulance, although the speedometer could tell the tale. I had devastating thoughts as I drove. I planned her funeral, selected the music in my mind and lined up the pallbearers. As I raced toward Pittsburgh it was obvious, at least in my mind, that this situation was going to have a tragic ending.

There's one question that continues to roam in my mind: Was I scared throughout Susan's ordeal? You bet I was! I thought how lonely it would be to come home and not find Sue there. How hard would it be to have our Sheltie, Regan, continue to whine and search rooms failing to find Sue? How lonely it would be to sit at the table alone. How empty it would be at night to not have her there to say at the end of each day "God bless you, I love you."

Who would select my clothes? She often said that clothes make the man—but without her help I'd be walking out looking like a clown. And I would miss her under-the-table shin kick at a social dinner advising me to keep my mouth shut.

I'd stare at the empty seat at Steelers' games. I'd miss her calling my name when out in the yard or upstairs in my office. I would miss our good-cop/bad-cop theatrics with car dealers. And surely I would miss her spaghetti sauce!

I'd miss her generosity and kindness toward others.

SUSAN EVANS

I would always cherish her love of Pittsburgh, her real home. I have never met anyone who loves this city as much as she does. Who would go to the Steelers' games with me and who would remind me, constantly, how great this team is?

Most of all, I'd miss her laughter and genuine sense of humor. I'd miss the scent of her perfume, the softness of her touch.

I'd miss an irresistible life with her that made me the luckiest man alive!

Was I scared about Sue's future? Need I answer the obvious? Even though there was a very positive medical prognosis, I still questioned. As good and experienced as these doctors are, did they still miss something? We all march when our Maker calls, but hopefully Sue's march will not be caused by her cancer. I had to trust the prognosis. Yet, life may take an unknown turn. That turn would really break my heart, not my faith, but my heart.

Am I thankful? You bet! I am thankful and grateful to Dr. Krivak and his staff, because in my mind they pulled off the miracle: Saving my wife's life. No one can ask for more. I truly trust them. He may not think of his work as a miracle—he told Sue that any doctor could have done what he did—but allow me to think that miracles do happen.

I am thankful to everyone who helped Sue and me along this journey. People from all walks of life, those whom I never thought would care.

Am I thankful for Susan, the love of my life? Need I answer that? We might be different in so many ways, yet we are the same.

But let us not forget that from that fateful day, June 13, 2012, all hell broke loose and our lives were changed forever. Again, you have to do what you have to do, whether married for 40 years or 40 days. As they say, once you think you've seen it all, wait until tomorrow.

I believe in hope, and I embrace it. Let the tomorrows take care of themselves.

SUSAN EVANS

"Fine"

And so the days and months flew by, I had never felt better. My treatments were finished, my marker number was "fine" (keep that word tucked in the back of your mind for a while) and it was time for another scan. The one in November of 2012 was "fine" and there was no reason to think that this one would be any different. However, I couldn't help but worry about this unknown result.

Before we go on let's look at the word "fine."

The literal definition—fine, finer, finest-means "excellent" or close to it. It may be a "fine" day outside or your flowers may be doing "fine" or you may feel "fine". We all know the connotation and the denotation of this very common word.

It's a word we understand. Again, just keep all of this "fine" information in an easily located space in your brain.

I worried about this test for two days. The scan would tell if all of this had been worth it and if I was good to go until the next scan. You learn that you live from one test result to another. Not a very peaceful way to live, but that's the way it is and I was beginning to believe that this would be the way it would be forever. There's that Sword of Damocles again.

The scan was uneventful and my local doctor told me I was "fine." He took the time to review the scan with George and I and pointed out all of my body parts (couldn't help but think the outline looked like a chicken ready to be stuffed) and also mentioned two small abnormalities which he sees in most women and that there was absolutely nothing to worry about. We left that appointment as happy as we had been in a long time. All was well, now we really could start living a normal life.

By now you know what happened.

We were wrong again!

The next day dawned sunny and beautiful. A perfect Fall day in Northwestern Pennsylvania. My husband and I had decided on a day trip to Niagara Falls to celebrate the good scan results. The sun was warm, the air cool, the sky blue. It doesn't get much better than this in October. We had planned a day of walking all around the Falls, some shopping and a stop for a nice dinner before driving home. We had even left the dog at doggie day-care, something we rarely did.

AND THEN THE CELL PHONE RANG.

As we crossed into New York State we couldn't help but marvel at the beauty of the day. The colorful leaves made us think that we were driving through a box of crayons.

And then the cell phone rang. (Who invented these things??)

Doctor Tom was calling to tell me that he saw two small abnormalities that probably were nothing (just as the other doctor had said) but he wouldn't be doing his job if he ignored them. There was a small nodule on my thyroid and a lymph node that he wanted checked. He wanted an ultrasound of the thyroid and a surgeon to check the lymph node. And then he said that maybe they would need to do a biopsy of the nodule.

I now understood what it meant when people said you can't sail without any wind. I had been sailing and now I abruptly was stopped. At that point I listened but couldn't breathe. He assured me that he thought it was going to be nothing to

SUSAN EVANS

worry about, but he wanted me to have the tests done just to be sure. Obviously, the day was ruined.

We continued to the Falls, my husband set on salvaging this day for me. We walked, I cried. We ate, I cried. We eliminated the shopping part of the day and returned home. Now those beautiful trees didn't look as wonderful as they had that morning.

It's always important to have someone check on things because when you can't breathe you really can't comprehend. George called Tom and received the same information as I had and the same assurances.

Even though I could be assured all day, it wasn't going to make me feel any better.

Then the lines of communication became taunt. I emailed Tom, he emailed back and said "not to worry." That's another phrase they must teach in medical school.

Not being one to accept anything I didn't like I emailed again, a rather terse email, wanting to know why the two doctors that he now would send me to were better than mine and why did I have to go through this hell. A rather terse phone call was the reply.

He was annoyed, of course, and he again explained that it was his job to make sure that nothing was wrong. I knew he was right but I was frightened, I think more frightened than I had been when I was originally diagnosed with ovarian cancer. The first time around I didn't know what to expect; this time I knew how bad the chemo treatments were and I wasn't about to think about doing any of that over again. He kept talking, I kept trying to interrupt but he didn't leave much room for my opinions. Did he even have any idea of how I felt? Why is it that doctors say they want you to question, but then when you do they get all pissed off????

I had been told that everything was "fine"—here it comes—he rather curtly informed me that "fine" was how he felt when he took his son to an expensive restaurant for dinner, it was not a clinician's term for a scan. I guess I had been told!

Of course he had the answers and I was going to do what he said (maybe if he would have "asked" I would have felt better)-there's that communication thing again.

I had to force myself to remember that this was just another annoyance and not a new tragedy.

Now two new doctors would be involved—he knew how I disliked most doctors and the entire medical process, but it had to be done.

SUSAN EVANS

So now I was being pawned off to two specialists. I had to take a few more days out of my schedule and drive to Pittsburgh. Again, I do not adjust well to change, especially when it is an opinion-driven change, but here I was looking at a pile of new patient paperwork.

Feeling that I was nearing my stress limit I had the ultrasound done in a small hospital. Now don't think everything was "fine" there either. When I got there they of course did not have my paperwork or even a work order. The young woman at the desk said, "Call your doctor and he will fax over the order." Now what if I didn't know the number? Luckily for me he now was on speed dial-and what if I had not had a cell phone? Perhaps, again, all of these people need some in-service training. Call I did and the order was promptly faxed. Can't anything ever be done right the first time??

I had worked myself up into just about a stress attack after the ultrasound. What if something really was wrong?

George and I had some time to spare before the next appointment and so we strolled through some shops and had breakfast. Not being real good with this cell phone technology I suddenly felt my handbag vibrate—a text message was there from my doctor who wanted to know how things were going and also wanted to reassure me again. That's the kind of care you need in these situations. There can be no substitute for a doctor who actually shows concern even when he is annoyed with you. But why is it when the person usually causing the worries (the doctor) is the person who always says not to worry?

The next stop was the surgeon who held my hand, told me nothing was wrong and gave me some excellent advice. He mentioned that he, too, was a cancer survivor and that I was not to worry every time I had an ache or pain that it was the cancer. He said that the only day to worry was the day I had a test or scan and to live my life all of the other days. Good advice, but not so easy to do.

The last stop was the ENT doctor who was going to check the thyroid. The waiting area was crowded, noisy and not very attractive, but I had no choice.

He checked my thyroid by putting tubes down my nostrils that could allow him to see the nodules. It seems that the one nodule on the CT scan was really three and he wanted the biopsy done. I knew I couldn't get through this day without a problem of some sort.

Now I reached my limit. The office worker who was going to call to set up my biopsy pushed me over the edge. She kept asking me, "How many nodules do you have?"

SUSAN EVANS

She was holding the paperwork but apparently she didn't understand something. I said "Two on the left and one on the right."

"But how many do you have?" she kept asking.

I kept answering, "Two on the left and one on the right."

She just wasn't getting it. The more she asked, in a very annoyed tone, the louder and more belligerent I got. Could she not add 2 and 1 and come up with 3? It seems like this math issue was following me throughout this journey.

Now that she really was annoyed with me and I with her, she tried to make my appointment for the biopsy. She was getting nowhere on that issue and so I suggested that she give me the phone and I could talk to the doctor in Olean, NY, myself. (She also couldn't understand the New York part and wondered if it bordered Pennsylvania!) I got nowhere with that request so I told her to just hang up. I took out my cell phone (right in front of the No Cell Phones Allowed sign) and I called the doctor on his cell phone. She was astounded that I would have a doctor's cell phone number. I didn't want to tell her that I had more than two in my "Contacts" app.

Appointment made, jump in the car and drive 3 1/2 hours home.

More stress, more emotions—and of course more crying. I started to wonder if this was quality of life or just quantity. This now was a side trip on my journey, not one that had been planned but sometimes one that happens.

Biopsy day came. Not a pleasant experience but one that was handled with great care and kindness and compassion by my Olean medical group. Dr. Ross Horsley was reassuring and the discomfort was short lived. With the help of Xanax I was relaxed and slept for the remainder of the day.

"Fine" was how I felt!

And now we just had to wait.

And wait we did for six days—that doesn't sound like an eternity, but when you're the one waiting for the results it seems like forever. And while I was waiting I was thinking the worst. Everyone tried to reassure me, but nothing helped.

AND WHILE I WAS WAITING I WAS THINKING THE WORST.

In the middle of this there was another appointment with my doctor. I was beginning to understand the "groupie" concept that followed rock bands. In order to see Dr. Tom I had to travel to parts of Pittsburgh that I had only

SUSAN EVANS

heard about on the news. Since he had various offices I had to find him.

The appointment was "fine" but there still were no test results. Don't think that anything ever moves quickly during this journey. The joke about "hurry up and wait" in the military carries over to the medical world as well.

When I again had to bring up the question of the tests I was informed that he was responsible for me and no one else. I wonder if he ever realized what a pain in the ass this responsibility could be.

I jokingly questioned him, however, about his choice of doctors that I had been assigned. The wonderful surgeon who gave me the cancer advice was a Bariatric surgeon and the ENT man had a sign in the office that advertised the days during which you could get Botox treatments. Now was this kind doctor of mine trying to tell me something? (He assured me he wasn't, but you never know what people really are thinking!)

The bottom line was that all the tests were negative and I was "fine." Imagine that!

The End Is Not Always the End

Well, here we are. You are almost ready to end this journey of mine. A year and a half has passed, a rather long time for a trip, and you have shared this sojourn with me from the beginning.

You shared my fears, hopefully you laughed a lot along the way as I did. And you saw that no matter how serious a situation, how hopeless it seems, there always is that light at the end of the tunnel. (We Pittsburghers know all about tunnels and how sometimes they can be an obstacle to a destination.)

So, you will close this book and hopefully you will better understand yourself or a friend who also has had to go on a trip of this nature. You may look back at some point and think, "That woman might have been nuts, but at least she laughed (when she wasn't crying) her way through a rather deplorable situation."

This trip, as life, required perseverance, tolerance, tenaciousness, inquisitiveness and assertiveness. Doesn't every unknown journey?

When you think you can't do anymore than you have done, you find out that you can.

I am sure that you have tried to follow your GPS system only to find that there is a detour that was never entered into the GPS "mother ship." It's very annoying, especially if you are in a hurry and have a shortage of time. Well, that's what cancer is—a detour in life's road. We will never have enough time and we're always in constant danger of running off the path, but if we stay the course we find ourselves back on the road and back on the track of life.

As your part of this journey is over, you'll put this book on a shelf as if you were putting your luggage back in the closet. The only difference is, your part of the journey is over and mine is not.

When my doctor told me that I would not be "cured" for five years I thought, "Good Lord, that's a very long time." My undergraduate work was only four years and that seemed like more than a lifetime to me!

But now more than one year has passed with no problems. Fifteen Avastin treatments seemed to be working. My CA125 number has remained between 6-11, excellent they tell me. Why it can't be zero is another one of the mysteries in this cancer business.

I feel wonderful. When people ask me how I feel I always reply, "I feel fine until someone tells me I'm not." That someone being my doctor. So far we're good. My tri-weekly exams are fine, my blood work is good. (Don't think it's easy having vaginal exams **TOMORROW WILL TAKE CARE OF ITSELF.** one day and then sitting across from this same doctor another day collaborating on this book. You can just throw being embarrassed and modest out of that proverbial window!)

I now take one day at a time—tomorrow will take care of itself.

I do feel, however, that I am on borrowed time, but aren't we all? Time seems to be running out, but isn't it always? I

SUSAN EVANS

often feel like Sisyphus the ancient mythological king who was condemned to pushing a giant boulder up a mountain. When he just about reaches the top the large rock would roll back to the bottom—he would never get the rock to the top. I may never feel 100% safe from this disease, but any percentage will be fine. (There's that word again, "fine.")

I want things done. The "to do" list always is in my hand and I get annoyed when anyone or anything slows me down.

Dealing with cancer and the treatments that go with it is difficult. It makes you a stronger person, remember people telling you all of your life, "what doesn't kill you will make you stronger?" Now I knew what they meant. I now was a survivor and now have to deal with different demons: check-ups, blood tests, scans, all of which can cause worry. After getting through the surgery and the chemotherapy with the love and support of my husband, friends and medical caregivers, I hopefully can be a person who gives a sense of joy to others who are starting or going through this journey. I feel that I have conquered, one day at a time, and I have won in so many ways.

And some "unimportant" things are still important in my life. I have attended Steelers' games in much better shape than last year. The walk from the parking lot to the stadium, which seemed like a marathon last year, is much more enjoyable this year. I still needed the suntan lotion but that was okay. When I entered that gate on opening day, 2013, tears were in my eyes. There were my football friends so happy to see me. "Dancing Robbie" climbed over a row of seats to kiss me and ask me how I was doing. He must have asked five times. Everyone was so supportive, and these were people who I hardly knew, except on Sundays.

I was back in the stadium, feeling great, and thinking of my father who had instilled this love of the team in me. As this season wore on I wondered why he had burdened me with this devotion to this team that for the first time in a long time was not doing well. Win or lose, you have to love 'em.

Mike the scan-man was right. I made it!

SUSAN EVANS

Epilogue

As I See It

As I look back on this on-going experience I see things a bit differently, or at least I see things!

Here goes…

It's not what happens to you in life, it's what you do about it.

If you follow the Bible and Jimmy Buffet's rules for life, you can't go wrong.

There are so few really nice men around that when you meet one, who is kind, and who also saved your life, you've hit the tri-fecta. Buy a lottery ticket.

The "fact" that dogs can be trained to sniff out ovarian cancer as reported in a local paper just might not be anything to bet on. Although I did see a report on the news one night that in Britain dogs are being trained to sniff breast cancer cells. I'm not sure about any of this. But what do I know? Perhaps you shouldn't run off and buy a dog as a precautionary measure.

You may think that you would get the most attention in a small hospital—not so. I found more care and compassion, understanding and empathy in the larger hospital. They have more experience in these serious medical problems and they understand what you're going through.

The quality of your health care always comes down to the quality of your doctors. Find the best ones you can.

Keep in mind—no matter how much we don't want to believe it—medicine is a business.

Doctors are not like the ones on the television show *Grey's Anatomy*. For one thing the scrubs are wrinkled—doesn't anyone own an iron anymore?

Insurance companies have a direct effect on your life, especially when they are at "war" with each other. If caught in the war, pick a side and hope for the best.

Sometimes when telling a story, even if it is your own, what you can say and what you want to say are two different things. It's unfortunate that some constructive criticism has to be neglected because of egos.

Listen to your doctor—not to the other patients in the chemo area. One patient told me that to have my incision close more quickly I shouldn't be doing what the doctor said and should be using wet tea bags instead. Earl Grey or English Breakfast??

You CAN disagree with your doctors. Just be ready for the backlash! Then, work with them, they know more than you.

Someone will always find you toilet tissue in the hospital.

Don't ever try to tell a teacher about lesson plans, unless you are a teacher.

Before you question why St. Francis and *Fifty Shades of Gray* are in the same chapter, you better read the life of Francis.

The end is not going to be tomorrow. It might take a while.

A kiss is just a kiss—but it might do wonders when you really need it.

Do doctors ever really enjoy those lovely homes they live in? Do they ever notice how beautiful the city looks at dawn while they're crossing a river to attend to an emergency? Do they ever just stop and live a normal life?

When you're feeling sorry for yourself remember that there are people having bigger problems than yours. While I was going through the worst of the chemo treatments, the East Coast was hit by Hurricane Sandy. Obviously I was pretty lucky lying in a warm bed with a roof over my head—those people affected by the storm weren't as lucky.

There is a Buddhist saying: "joyfully participate in the sorrows of life." With cancer, you have no choice but to participate if you are going to get well, so you might as well do it joyfully.

In all due respect to my white-coated friends—always, and I mean always—remember—God saves lives—you're just his helpers.

No words of thanks can ever be enough for the people who took such good care of me throughout this journey.

Acknowledgements

There are no words that could thank all of the people who have been with me through this journey, some of whom have been mentioned in this book. However, there are some who need extra thanks.

To Father Leo Gallina and Father Ray Gramata who were there at the beginning of this journey.

Dr. F. Price, Barbara Thomas, Patricia A. Johnson, RN,BSN,CNOR, Deb Linhart who made my tour of the West Penn operating rooms possible.

Dr. M. Javed Akhtar and his wife Shahnaz who encouraged me when I really needed it.

Dr. Luis Gonzalez and Dr. Nancy Fuhrman who knew I didn't "just" have a swollen ankle.

The people at the Canonsburg Hospital who allowed me to observe a surgery.

Crystalyn Schmidt, Lynne Hahn, Heather English and Danielle Robison who made my clinic and office visits bearable.

Chris Binger, Nora Lersch, and Karen Lyle my tri-weekly PA's who assured me that I was doing "fine".

Jim Tingley who walked and pushed me through using Microsoft Word. His patience was incredible.

Dr. Mike Felix who gave me such good advice about coping with a life with cancer.

Fran and Judy Rovito who became our "property managers" and took care of our home while we were away so often.

Fran Rovito who unknowingly gave us the title to this book.

George and Shirley Johnson who offered support every step of the way.

William Chapman whose constant concern, calls and friendship made this a bit more bearable.

Everyone at the University of Pittsburgh at Bradford who called, sent numerous floral arrangements, emails, notes and words of encouragement.

To the two women who were always there-Kathy Kresge and Barb Kilpatrick-their constant encouragement and support got me through some of the worst days.

And to the two men who have gotten me through this journey, one who has been by my side for 40 years and who showed remarkable courage, strength, compassion and understanding and love—my husband George.

The other, a man who just strolled into my life and had the skill to save it—my doctor, and friend, Tom Krivak. His compassion, understanding and sense of responsibility made me feel safe and instilled in me the belief that this would all be "fine." Hopefully he will be here for 40 more years.

SUSAN EVANS

Long Art Company

Biography for
SUSAN EVANS

Susan Evans was a secondary English and Remedial Reading teacher for 32 years in Bradford, PA. She co-advised the award–winning high school yearbook, *The Barker*, taught yearbook classes and judged yearbooks for the Columbia Scholastic Press Association, for which she was awarded the Gold Key from Columbia University.

When she retired in 2002, she was recognized by the Pennsylvania Senate and Sen. Joseph Scarnati with a special citation for her instructional devotion.

Evans, a native of Pittsburgh, PA, earned a Master's degree in secondary education from St. Bonaventure University and a Bachelor's degree in education from Slippery Rock University. She also holds a certificate in Drug and Alcohol Counseling from Penn State University.

She is a past Bradford Rotary Club president and a Paul Harris Fellow and a current member of the Advisory Board of the University of Pittsburgh at Bradford. The Evanses are also members of the Brackenridge Circle at the University of Pittsburgh.

Susan and her husband George and Regan, the run-away dog, have residences in Bradford and Cranberry Township, PA.

Joshua Franzos Photography

Biography for
THOMAS C. KRIVAK, M.D.

Thomas C. Krivak, M.D., is a gynecological oncologist in Pittsburgh, PA. His medical school education was at the Ohio State College of Medicine and his training in Gynecological Oncology was performed at the Walter Reed Army Medical Center and the National Cancer Institute. He served in the U.S. Air Force from 1994–2005 as a military physician.

While in Pittsburgh, Dr. Krivak has focused his research on women with gynecologic cancers developing personalized treatment plans using molecular profiling of a patient's tumor. Additionally, his research has evaluated the use of aggressive surgery and surgical techniques for women with gynecological cancers.

He serves as co-director of the Society of Gynecologic Oncology Research Institute, and has presented numerous research articles and has over 75 peer reviewed publications, numerous book chapters and research presentations.

Dr. Krivak provides care for women in the Western Pennsylvania area and is employed by the Allegheny Health Network. He serves as co-director of the Division of Gynecologic Oncology and director of women's cancer research within the division.

WA